THE POWER OF GOD

The Word That Will Change Your Life Today

EDWARD D. ANDREWS

THE POWER OF GOD

The Word That Will Change Your Life Today

Edward D. Andrews

Christian Publishing House
Cambridge, Ohio

Copyright © 2018 Edward D. Andrews

All rights reserved. Except for brief quotations in articles, other publications, book reviews, and blogs, no part of this book may be reproduced in any manner without prior written permission from the publishers. For information, write, support@christianpublishers.org

Unless otherwise stated, Scripture quotations are from Updated American Standard Version (UASV) Copyright © 2022 by Christian Publishing House

THE POWER OF GOD: The Word That Will Change Your Life Today by Edward D. Andrews

ISBN-10: 1945757892

ISBN-13: 978-1945757891

Table of Contents

Book Description 9
Preface 11
Introduction 13
Chapter 1: In the Beginning: God's Power to Create 15
    1.1 Understanding God's Power in Creation 15
    1.2 The Grandeur of the Universe: God's Artistry 17
    1.3 God's Design in the Animal Kingdom: A Display of Power 19
    1.4 Humanity: The Crown of Creation 21
    1.5 The Restorative Power of God in Creation 23
    1.6 The Harmony of Creation: Indicative of Divine Order 25
Chapter 2: God Destroys: God's Power to Judge 27
    2.1 The Great Flood: Judgment and Mercy 27
    2.2 The Destruction of Sodom and Gomorrah: Righteous Judgment 29
    2.3 Pharaoh's Downfall: A Display of God's Power 31
    2.4 The Canaanite Conquest: God's Power in Action 33
    2.5 The Babylonian Exile: A Lesson in Humility 34
    2.6 God's Judgment: A Call to Righteous Living 36
Chapter 3: The Almighty Shield: God's Power to Protect. 39
    3.1 The Exodus: A Mighty Display of Protection 39
    3.2 Daniel in the Lion's Den: Unseen Shields 42
    3.3 The Preservation of the Remnant: God's Protective Hand 44
    3.4 God's Power in Spiritual Warfare 47
    3.5 Our Refuge and Strength: Personal Experiences of God's Protection 49

3.6 The Ultimate Protection: The Promise of Eternal Life 51

Chapter 4: Redeemed: God's Power to Restore 54

4.1 The Prodigal Son: A Parable of Restoration 54

4.2 Job's Restoration: Triumph Over Trials 56

4.3 The Resurrection of Lazarus: A Glimpse of Restorative Power 58

4.4 Spiritual Restoration: From Death to Life 60

4.5 Spiritual Israel: Christians Are Now God's People 63

4.6 Spiritual Regeneration (Palingenesia): A New Life in the Sinful Person 65

Chapter 5: Our Part: Sharing in the Power of God 67

5.1 Understanding Our Position: Clay in the Potter's Hands 67

5.2 Aligning with God's Will: The First Step to Power 69

5.3 Active Faith: A Catalyst for Divine Power 71

5.4 The Power of Prayer: Communicating with the Divine ... 73

5.5 The Bible: The Word of God Exerts Power 75

5.6 Serving Others: Demonstrating God's Power in Us 77

Chapter 6: Harnessing the Power: The Word That Changes Lives 80

6.1 God's Word: A Powerful Weapon 80

6.2 The Transformative Power of the Scriptures 82

6.3 Meditating on the Word: Key to Spiritual Growth 84

6.4 In-Depth Study of God's Word: Getting at What the Bible Authors Meant by the Word that They Used 87

6.5 Living Out the Word: A Daily Challenge 89

6.6 The Word of God and You: The Bible Is Authentic and True 91

Chapter 7: The Divine Blueprint: God's Power in His Laws 94

7.1 Understanding God's Laws: A Reflection of His Power ..94

7.2 The Ten Commandments: The Pillars of God's Authority 97

7.3 Laws of Love: God's Power in Relationships 99

7.4 God's Laws: Let God's Laws and Principles Train Your Conscience 101

7.5 Prophetic Laws: God's Sovereign Power Over Time 103

7.6 God's Moral Laws: The Power of Righteous Living 106

Chapter 8: Divine Intervention: God's Power in History. 108

8.1 Egypt to Canaan: God's Power Over Nations 108

8.2 The Fall of Babylon: God's Sovereignty 110

8.3 Rise of Persia: God's Hand in Global Affairs 113

8.4 The Arrival of the Messiah: Fulfillment of Prophecy 115

8.5 The Early Church: God's Power in Persecution............. 117

8.6 Modern-Day Spiritual Israel: God's Power in Restoration 120

Chapter 9: Walking in Wisdom: God's Power in Discernment............123

9.1 Solomon's Wisdom: A Gift from Above......................... 123

9.2 Discerning Good from Evil: God's Power in Moral Judgments............ 125

9.3 The Wisdom in Proverbs: God's Power for Daily Living 127

9.4 Discerning God's Will: The Power of Divine Guidance 130

9.5 Wisdom in Suffering: The Power of God in Trials 132

9.6 The Wisdom of Christ: God's Power for Redemption .. 135

Chapter 10: Eternal Promises: God's Power in Salvation. 138

10.1 The Promise of the Messiah: A Display of Redemptive Power 138

10.2 Christ's Resurrection: The Ultimate Demonstration of God's Power.. 140

10.3 The Gift of Grace: God's Power to Save......................... 142

10.4 The Mind of Christ: God's Power in Our Lives............. 144

10.5 The Second Coming: God's Promised Future................ 146

10.6 The New Jerusalem: God's Power in Our Eternal Hope 148

BIBLIOGRAPHY 151

Book Description

In "THE POWER OF GOD: The Word That Will Change Your Life Today," esteemed Bible author Andrews explores the awe-inspiring manifestations of God's power as reflected in the Scriptures and in our lives today. This riveting journey starts from the first pages of Genesis, where God's creative power shaped the universe, and concludes with the prophecies of an eternal future under His divine providence.

Throughout this deeply inspiring and life-altering work, Andrews demonstrates how God's power, which is capable of creating, judging, protecting, and restoring, infuses courage and hope into our lives. God's "extraordinary power" is not only a testament of His authority and might but is also a reassurance of His boundless love for those who serve Him.

The book further delves into understanding the divine blueprint through God's laws, showcasing how His power shapes our moral and ethical frameworks. Andrews unveils God's interventions throughout history, His power in granting wisdom and discernment, and the eternal promise of salvation. He invites readers to discover their strengths, abilities, and potential in harnessing God's power in their walk of faith.

This illuminating work aims to empower readers, enriching their lives with divine wisdom and understanding. It challenges the reader to rise to a new level of spiritual maturity and invites them to experience God's transformative power through His Word, the ultimate guide to spiritual growth.

"THE POWER OF GOD: The Word That Will Change Your Life Today" serves as a beacon of hope and strength, assuring readers that God's protective power is always working to ensure the outworking of His will and purpose, not only in the cosmic plan but also in the intimate details of our personal lives. Andrews provides profound insights that lead to a deeper relationship with God—a journey that is filled with hope, strength, wisdom, and the promise of eternal life.

Preface

The omnipotence of God is a subject that has captivated the minds of believers throughout history. It's a theme woven into the fabric of our faith, a tenet central to understanding the character of the Almighty. "THE POWER OF GOD: The Word That Will Change Your Life Today" is born out of a deep fascination with this divine attribute and an earnest desire to help others grasp its implications in their spiritual journey.

My primary objective in writing this book is not simply to reiterate the fact that God is powerful—this truth, after all, is accepted by anyone who acknowledges God. Rather, my goal is to explore the specific ways God's power has been manifest throughout history, how it is evident in His laws and His acts of judgment and grace, and, most importantly, how it can be made manifest in our own lives.

This book is not a detached, academic treatise on divine omnipotence. It is a deeply personal work, for it arises from my own experiences with God's power, from those moments of despair when His strength became my refuge, to the times of joy and celebration when His creative and restorative power was evident in ways large and small. It is my hope that by sharing these experiences, combined with a meticulous study of the Bible, I can help readers not only understand God's power on a deeper level but also experience it in a more profound and personal way.

In this work, I've sought to uphold the integrity and inerrancy of the Scriptures, using them as the ultimate guide and reference. I've approached each verse, each biblical account, with reverence and humility, conscious of the fact that any human interpretation is fallible and that the fullness of divine revelation can never be entirely comprehended by the human mind.

As you read this book, my prayer is that you will feel a sense of awe and wonder at the power of our God, that you will be moved to delve deeper into the Scriptures, and that you will be inspired to invite

God's extraordinary power into your life. And, ultimately, I hope that this exploration of God's power will embolden your walk with Him, transforming your faith from something you have into something you live, every day.

Edward D. Andrews

EDWARD D. ANDREWS (AS in Criminal Justice, BS in Religion, MA in Biblical Studies, and MDiv in Theology) is CEO and President of Christian Publishing House. He has authored over 220+ books. In addition, Andrews is the Chief Translator of the Updated American Standard Version (UASV).

Introduction

Every journey has a starting point. For some, the journey into understanding and experiencing the power of God begins in a moment of profound need. For others, it's a path entered due to an insatiable curiosity to understand the divine or a deep-seated desire for spiritual growth. Regardless of the reasons that have led you to open this book, my hope is that by the end, you'll have a richer and deeper understanding of God's power, and how it can truly change your life today.

The power of God is not an abstract concept meant only for theologians to ponder. It's a living, dynamic force that has tangible impacts on our world, on our lives, and on our personal spiritual journeys. This book aims to take these profound divine truths and bring them into our everyday human experience.

Throughout the chapters that follow, we'll delve into a multitude of biblical accounts—stories of creation, destruction, protection, and restoration—all testifying to the multifaceted power of God. These stories, filled with awe-inspiring demonstrations of God's power, are not just ancient history; they are narratives that hold the potential to transform our understanding and experience of God's power in the here and now.

Moreover, we'll consider how God's power is displayed in His divine laws, in His intervention throughout history, in His gift of wisdom, and most beautifully, in His promise of salvation. In each of these aspects, we will see not only the power of God but also His goodness, His love, His justice, and His mercy.

Importantly, this book isn't just about observing God's power from a distance. It's about drawing close, about personal engagement, and about the transformation that comes when we truly start to understand and engage with God's power in our own lives. It's about the word of God—alive, powerful, sharper than any two-edged sword—transforming us from the inside out.

As we embark on this journey together, my hope is that you won't just learn about the power of God, but that you'll experience it. That you will see His power in the world around you, that you will feel His power in your own life, and that you'll be inspired to live out that power in service to Him and to others.

Prepare to be transformed by THE POWER OF GOD: The Word That Will Change Your Life Today.

Chapter 1: In the Beginning: God's Power to Create

1.1 Understanding God's Power in Creation

The exploration of God's power must begin where the biblical narrative starts – with creation. The book of Genesis opens with a succinct yet profoundly impactful statement, "In the beginning God created the heavens and the earth" (Genesis 1:1, ASV). This simple declaration carries within it a depth of understanding about God's power that can significantly change our perspective of Him and His relationship with us.

The act of creation is perhaps the most vivid display of God's power. The word used for God in Genesis 1:1 is the Hebrew term 'Elohim,' which captures the essential nature of God's power. It is plural in form, but used with singular verbs and adjectives when referring to the One true God, suggesting the magnitude of His power and majesty.

This inaugural verse, so potent in its simplicity, doesn't dwell on explaining how the universe was created, but it makes a point to let us know by whom. And, it is the 'Who' that matters. This verse anchors our understanding of the world around us in the knowledge that an omnipotent God initiated everything that exists. He wasn't a divine sculptor who needed pre-existing material to shape the world, but the Almighty Creator who summoned the universe into existence ex nihilo, or "out of nothing."

God's act of creation, in essence, goes beyond physical formation; it touches every fabric of existence, visible and invisible. He created time – the "beginning," space – the "heavens," and matter – the "earth." In the Hebrew mindset, these three aspects encapsulate the totality of the universe. Hence, God's power is not merely over the universe, but His power is what brought the universe into being.

As we progress through Genesis 1, we encounter a powerful rhythmic pattern: "And God said, Let there be...and there was..." (Genesis 1:3, ASV). The original language indicates a command or decree, highlighting God's authoritative power. His words were not just descriptive; they were creative and productive. This pattern of divine fiats underscores that God's word itself is imbued with His power, a theme resonating throughout the scriptures.

As we further examine God's power in creation, we are introduced to an aspect of His nature – God as a life-giver. God didn't just create inanimate matter; He breathed life into His creation, most notably into mankind. "And the LORD God formed man of the dust of the ground, and breathed into his nostrils the breath of life; and man became a living soul" (Genesis 2:7, ASV). Here, we see God's life-giving power at its zenith. He did not just create human beings; He created us in His image and likeness (Genesis 1:27, ASV), bestowing upon us a reflection of His attributes, including the capacity to reason, feel, create, and make moral judgments.

This act of imparting life is significant because it sets God apart from His creation, demonstrating that while everything else is dependent, God is self-existent – an attribute theologians refer to as 'aseity.' This self-existence underscores God's power as not merely superior to, but qualitatively different from, any power that creatures might possess.

But, God's power in creation does not end in Genesis. It is an ongoing process, a continual demonstration of His active presence in the world. The Psalmist declares, "The heavens declare the glory of God, and the sky above proclaims his handiwork" (Psalm 19:1, ESV). Every sunrise, every starry sky, every change in seasons is a testament to God's unceasing creative power.

Recognizing God's power in creation is not merely a matter of marveling at the vastness of the cosmos or the intricacy of DNA. It is a call to acknowledge God as the sole and sovereign Creator who, in His power, not only created but continues to sustain everything by the power of His word (Hebrews 1:3, ESV). It is to affirm that the Creator-God is distinct from His creation, not part of it, transcending both time and space. Moreover, it is a call to recognize and appreciate our unique position as creatures made in God's image and the stewardship responsibilities that come with that status.

By understanding God's power in creation, we acquire a profound appreciation for His might, not as a remote or impersonal force, but as a purposeful and relational divine Person. Recognizing the power of God in creation helps us perceive our own weakness and need for His strength in our lives. It underscores that God, who had the power to create the universe, has the power to intervene in our lives, to change circumstances, and to make all things new. This realization can change our life today.

To understand God's power in creation is to affirm the words of the Apostle Paul: "For from him and through him and to him are all things. To him be glory forever. Amen" (Romans 11:36, ESV). It is an acknowledgment that places God rightly at the center of our lives and our universe, a perspective that will indeed change your life today.

1.2 The Grandeur of the Universe: God's Artistry

When we seek to comprehend the grandeur of the universe, we inevitably encounter the artistry of God. Psalm 19:1 (ESV) tells us, "The heavens declare the glory of God, and the sky above proclaims his handiwork." The grandeur of the universe, in all its magnitude and minute details, is a testament to the power and creativity of God, the ultimate artist.

The cosmos, in all its complexity and beauty, eloquently speaks of God's artistry. From the smallest subatomic particle to the vast array of galaxies, every element of creation reflects God's creative power. The universe is not the result of chance or random processes but is the deliberate and purposeful act of a powerful Creator.

Consider the earth's position in the solar system, precisely poised at the perfect distance from the sun. Too close, and it would be scorched. Too far away, and it would be a frozen wasteland. This "Goldilocks zone" allows for a diverse array of life and ecosystems, a stunning showcase of God's creative brilliance.

Even the complexity and variety of life on earth speak volumes about God's creative power. The multitude of species, each with unique characteristics and ecosystems they inhabit, reflect a Creator who delights in diversity and complexity. Whether it's the iridescent scales of a butterfly or the intricate systems that keep our bodies functioning, we see God's artistry on display.

In the vastness of the universe, we find galaxies, each containing millions or even billions of stars. The Hubble Space Telescope has given us breathtaking images of these distant star clusters, a celestial ballet of light and color. The psalmist writes, "When I consider your heavens, the work of your fingers, the moon and the stars, which you have set in place" (Psalm 8:3, ESV), we get a glimpse into the grandeur and beauty that God has woven into the very fabric of the cosmos.

Yet God's artistry is not only about grand scales and complex systems. It's also seen in the smallest of details. Take the human body, for instance. Our DNA, the blueprint for our individuality, is a marvel of divine artistry. Comprised of about 3 billion base pairs, if unwound and linked together, it would reach from the earth to the sun and back more than 300 times. Within this intricate molecular structure lies the programming for every aspect of our physical being.

Moreover, the synchronization of various bodily systems working in harmony demonstrates an elegance that surpasses any symphony. This delicate, intricate design of the human body bears the unmistakable signature of a master designer.

The grandeur of the universe, therefore, is not a testimony to impersonal cosmic forces, but the creative prowess of a purposeful God. It's a testament to His boundless imagination and meticulous attention to detail.

Beyond the physical realm, God's artistry also extends to moral and spiritual dimensions. By creating humans in His image (Genesis 1:27, ASV), God has imparted a moral consciousness, a sense of right and wrong, that sets us apart from the rest of the animal kingdom. Furthermore, God has planted eternity in our hearts (Ecclesiastes 3:11, ASV), a yearning for something beyond the physical world. This intrinsic moral and spiritual dimension is a testament to God's artistry at a level that transcends the physical universe.

Understanding the grandeur of the universe and seeing it as a reflection of God's artistry provides us with a renewed sense of awe and respect for our Creator. It shifts our perspective from a mundane, earthly focus to a divine, heavenly one. It reminds us of our place in this vast universe and of the God who created and sustains it all with His extraordinary power.

1.3 God's Design in the Animal Kingdom: A Display of Power

The animal kingdom, in all its complexity and diversity, serves as a profound testament to God's creative power. Each animal, from the tiniest insect to the largest mammal, bears the mark of His divine design. His ability to create such a myriad of creatures, each perfectly adapted to its environment, illustrates His immeasurable power and foresight.

Consider the diversity that exists within the animal kingdom. Scientists have identified over 8.7 million different species on earth, each one unique in its form and function. This figure doesn't even include the countless species that have yet to be discovered. Each species has its own set of characteristics that distinguish it from all others, an undeniable display of God's creative ability.

God's design in the animal kingdom is not merely aesthetic, it's functional. Animals have been equipped with an array of features that allow them to thrive in their specific environments. For instance, camels have humps to store fat, which they can convert into water and energy during long periods without food or water. Polar bears have a layer of blubber for insulation against the extreme cold, and a white fur coat that provides camouflage in the snow.

The bird kingdom offers a glimpse into God's innovative designs. Take, for instance, the hummingbird, the only bird that can fly backwards. It has a high metabolism to maintain its rapid wing movement, and a unique skeletal structure that allows for this unparalleled mobility. Such intricate design points to a Creator who is not just powerful, but also imaginative and detail-oriented.

In the marine world, the design of the dolphin exemplifies God's wisdom. Dolphins have a streamlined shape for efficient movement in water, a blowhole on top of their heads for easy breathing while swimming, and a complex sonar system for navigation and hunting. These features are not the product of random processes, but the design of a wise and powerful Creator.

It's not just the physical design of animals that reflects God's power, but also their instinctive behaviors. Take the monarch butterfly, for instance. Every year, these butterflies migrate thousands of miles from North America to Mexico - a journey that no single butterfly has made before, since the butterflies that return are the great-grandchildren of the butterflies that left. Yet, they instinctively know the path to navigate. This internal GPS system, ingrained within their genetic code, is a testament to God's foresight and intricate design.

Scripture also highlights God's power as displayed in the animal kingdom. In the book of Job, God Himself points out the features of various creatures to highlight His creative power (Job 39, ASV). He speaks about the mountain goats giving birth, the wild donkey's freedom, the ostrich's peculiar behavior, the horse's strength, and the eagle's ability to spot its prey from afar. In all these examples, God is illustrating His power, wisdom, and the deliberation that went into the creation of each creature.

In the New Testament, Jesus uses birds to teach an important lesson about God's providence. "Look at the birds of the air: they neither sow nor reap nor gather into barns, and yet your heavenly Father feeds them. Are you not of more value than they?" (Matthew 6:26, ESV). Here, Jesus is pointing to God's provision for even the smallest and most seemingly insignificant creatures as evidence of His care and attention to detail.

In conclusion, the animal kingdom stands as a testament to God's creative power and design. It showcases His attention to detail, His care for His creation, and His power to create a diverse array of creatures, each perfectly adapted to its environment. As we explore the intricacies of the animal kingdom, we gain a deeper appreciation for our powerful Creator and His remarkable creation.

1.4 Humanity: The Crown of Creation

While the magnificence of the universe and the complexity of the animal kingdom stand as testaments to God's creative power, there is one aspect of creation that distinctly bears His image—humankind. The creation of humanity is the pinnacle of God's creative work, an expression of His power, wisdom, and relational nature.

The creation account in Genesis tells us that God created man and woman in His own image (Genesis 1:27, ASV). This doesn't mean that we physically resemble God, who is spirit (John 4:24, ESV), but rather, that we bear His likeness in our moral, spiritual, rational, relational, and creative capacities. Unlike other creatures, humans have the ability to think abstractly, appreciate beauty, create, make moral judgments, and cultivate relationships with each other and with God.

The distinctiveness of human beings is underscored by the specific attention God gave to their creation. While God merely spoke other elements of creation into existence, He formed man from the dust of the ground and breathed into his nostrils the breath of life (Genesis 2:7, ASV). Moreover, God personally planted a garden in Eden for the man to live in, showing His intentional provision and care (Genesis 2:8, ASV).

Another element that sets humans apart is their dominion over creation. God entrusted them with the responsibility to "rule over the fish in the sea and the birds in the sky, over the livestock and all the wild animals, and over all the creatures that move along the ground" (Genesis 1:26, ASV). This mandate reflects humans' unique position in creation and emphasizes their role as stewards of God's earth.

The creation of humanity also reflects God's relational nature. It is within the context of humanity that God chose to reveal Himself, interact, and establish a covenant relationship. Genesis 3:8, ASV, depicts God walking in the garden in the cool of the day, highlighting the intimate relationship He had with Adam and Eve. This relational aspect sets humanity apart as the crown of creation.

Furthermore, human beings were created with free will, a concept that ties in with God's foreknowledge and the notion of human freedom. God, in His omniscience, knows in advance what individuals will freely choose. Yet, His foreknowledge doesn't compromise or dictate human free will. Humans, unlike other creatures, have the freedom to make choices and determine their actions.

Moreover, the human capacity for spirituality marks another distinctive aspect of our creation. Humans have an innate longing for the divine, a sense of morality, and a desire for purpose and meaning that can only be satisfied in a relationship with their Creator. This is beautifully expressed in Ecclesiastes 3:11, ASV: "He hath made everything beautiful in its time: also he hath set eternity in their heart."

Lastly, human beings are the only part of creation for whom God has made provisions for redemption. Despite our fall into sin, God, in His love, provided a way of salvation through Jesus Christ. John 3:16, ESV, declares, "For God so loved the world, that he gave his only Son, that whoever believes in him should not perish but have eternal life."

In conclusion, the creation of humanity showcases God's power, wisdom, and relational nature. From our distinctive abilities to our entrusted dominion and our unique spiritual dimension, we see that humans are indeed the crown of God's creation. This understanding should inspire us to fulfill our God-given role as stewards, to live in relationship with our Creator, and to appreciate the worth and dignity of every human being. For in understanding our place in creation, we gain a deeper appreciation for the Creator Himself.

1.5 The Restorative Power of God in Creation

While God's initial act of creation beautifully displays His omnipotence, His ongoing work in creation and His promises for the future vividly manifest His restorative power. The narrative of Scripture portrays God not only as a Creator but also as a Redeemer, a God who restores and renews what has been broken and marred by sin.

Sin's entry into the world brought chaos and destruction, affecting not just humanity but the entire creation. Romans 8:20-22, ASV, describes creation as being subjected to futility, groaning, and suffering the pains of childbirth, yearning for a release from the curse of sin. Yet, even in this state of disorder, we see God's restorative power at work.

One of the earliest indications of God's intention to restore His creation can be seen in His response to Adam and Eve's disobedience. Despite their rebellion, God made garments of skins for Adam and his wife and clothed them (Genesis 3:21, ASV), a gesture that signified God's commitment to their well-being and a foreshadowing of the ultimate covering of sin through the sacrifice of Christ.

God's redemptive power is not limited to humanity but encompasses the entire cosmos. This is evident in His covenant with Noah following the flood. In Genesis 9:11, ASV, God declares, "And I will establish my covenant with you; neither shall all flesh be cut off any more by the waters of the flood; neither shall there any more be a flood to destroy the earth." This promise demonstrates God's commitment to preserve the earth despite the pervasiveness of human sin.

Moreover, God's restorative power is vividly displayed through the nation of Israel. Despite their repeated rebellion, God continually brought them back from the brink of destruction. This pattern of judgment followed by restoration underscores God's steadfast love and His commitment to His promises.

The pinnacle of God's restorative work, however, is seen in the person and work of Jesus Christ. In Him, God provided the ultimate solution to the problem of sin. Jesus' death and resurrection not only reconcile sinful humanity to God but also pave the way for the restoration of all things. As Colossians 1:20, ESV, states, "and through him to reconcile to himself all things, whether on earth or in heaven, making peace by the blood of his cross."

This promise of cosmic restoration finds its ultimate fulfillment in the eschatological vision of a new heaven and a new earth depicted in Revelation 21:1, ASV, "And I saw a new heaven and a new earth: for the first heaven and the first earth have passed away; and the sea is no more." Here, the created order is not abandoned but renewed, redeemed, and restored to its intended glory, free from the effects of sin and death.

Even in the present, we can see God's restorative power at work. Through the Holy Spirit-inspired word, believers are transformed and renewed, growing into the likeness of Christ. As Romans 12:2, ESV, urges, "Do not be conformed to this world, but be transformed by the renewal of your mind."

God's restorative power is also evidenced in the Christian community's call to participate in His restorative work. Believers, as ambassadors of Christ, are called to preach the reconciliation message, to love and serve others, and to steward the earth responsibly, anticipating the day when all things will be made new.

In conclusion, God's restorative power in creation paints a picture of a God who, in His mercy and love, not only creates but also sustains and renews His creation. Despite the pervasive effects of sin, God has set in motion a plan for restoration that encompasses the entire cosmos, culminating in a new heaven and a new earth where righteousness dwells. This grand narrative of creation, fall, redemption, and restoration powerfully testifies to the steadfast love, justice, and restorative power of our Creator God.

1.6 The Harmony of Creation: Indicative of Divine Order

God's creation is not a chaotic jumble of elements, but an intricate tapestry woven with precision and purpose. This harmony is not a random occurrence but indicative of divine order, reflecting the character of an orderly, meticulous, and purposeful Creator.

When examining the Genesis creation account, one immediately notes the structured progression of events (Genesis 1, ASV). The world is not haphazardly formed; instead, each creation day lays the groundwork for the next. Light precedes the formation of light-bearers (the sun, moon, and stars); the separation of waters and the emergence of dry land sets the stage for the creation of plant life, and so forth. This orderly progression signifies God's wisdom and understanding in laying out His creative work.

Beyond this sequential order, the creation account also highlights balance and symmetry, reinforcing the concept of divine harmony. For instance, the first three days of creation dealing with forms (light and darkness, sea and sky, land and vegetation) are paralleled by the next three days dealing with their respective rulers or inhabitants (sun and moon, birds and fish, land animals and humans). This pattern underscores a balance that resonates with God's character of precision and balance.

The very nature of the universe, with its physical laws and constants, points to an ordered creation. From the intricacies of atomic structures to the vast expanse of the cosmos, everything operates according to established laws that ensure stability and predictability. The regularity of the seasons, the precision of an eclipse, the delicate balance of ecosystems, all attest to a world imbued with divine order (Jeremiah 33:25, ASV).

In addition to physical harmony, God's creation also exhibits a moral order. The moral laws given by God reflect His holy character and provide a framework for human relationships and societal structures. They point us to what is good and righteous, echoing the character of a holy and just Creator.

Moreover, the harmony of creation is manifested in the interconnectedness and interdependence of all living things. Every creature, no matter how small, has a role in the grand scheme of life. This concept, known as the web of life, points to a complex, interconnected system designed with foresight and purpose.

The pinnacle of this divine harmony, however, is seen in humanity, the crown of God's creation. Created in God's image (Genesis 1:27, ASV), humans have the unique capacity to relate to God and to reflect His character. They were given dominion over the earth (Genesis 1:28, ASV), entrusted with the responsibility to steward God's creation in a way that reflects His wisdom and order.

Sadly, the introduction of sin disrupted the harmony of God's creation. However, the Gospel provides a means for the restoration of this broken harmony. Through Christ's redemptive work on the cross, humanity is reconciled to God, and the entire creation awaits the final restoration of harmony and peace (Romans 8:19-23, ESV).

In summary, the harmony seen in the cosmos is a reflection of the Creator's character—His wisdom, His orderliness, His precision, and His purposefulness. It serves as a constant reminder of His omnipotence and wisdom, providing a glimpse into the mind of our Creator God. This harmony is not just an abstract concept but a divine reality that calls us to live in harmony with our Creator, with each other, and with the rest of creation.

Chapter 2: God Destroys: God's Power to Judge

2.1 The Great Flood: Judgment and Mercy

The biblical account of the Great Flood is a pivotal narrative that underscores God's power to judge, whilst simultaneously highlighting His mercy. This incident, described vividly in Genesis 6-9 (ASV), signifies both God's intolerance towards human wickedness and His gracious provision for salvation.

The backdrop to the flood is a world steeped in sin. Genesis 6:5 (ASV) poignantly observes, "And Jehovah saw that the wickedness of man was great in the earth, and that every imagination of the thoughts of his heart was only evil continually." It was a time marked by pervasive moral corruption and violence, which necessitated divine intervention.

In this dark hour, God exercised His power to judge. In His righteousness, He could not ignore or tolerate the overwhelming wickedness. Genesis 6:7 (ASV) states, "And Jehovah said, I will destroy man whom I have created from the face of the ground; both man, and beast, and creeping things, and birds of the heavens; for it repenteth me that I have made them."

Yet, amidst judgment, God's mercy shone bright. Noah found grace in the eyes of the Lord (Genesis 6:8, ASV). He was a just man, and perfect in his generations, one who walked with God (Genesis 6:9, ASV). Here, God's omniscient foreknowledge of Noah's righteousness, not infringing on Noah's free will, plays a crucial role in the narrative.

God revealed His plan to Noah, instructing him to construct an ark for the preservation of his household and representatives of all living creatures. Noah obeyed, demonstrating faith in God's word, though the impending judgment was yet unseen. This narrative illustrates how God's foreknowledge of human actions, rooted in their free will, works in concert with His divine plan.

The flood narrative displays God's sovereignty over the natural world as He manipulated natural elements to execute His judgment, causing it to rain forty days and forty nights (Genesis 7:12, ASV). Yet, the same waters of judgment were also waters of salvation for Noah and his family, safely housed in the ark.

After the floodwaters receded, God made a covenant with Noah and all living creatures, signified by the rainbow, promising never again to destroy the earth by a flood (Genesis 9:11-16, ASV). This first biblical covenant, both universal and unconditional, again underlined God's mercy even after executing judgment.

Moreover, Noah's post-flood actions - building an altar and offering sacrifices to God - were a fitting response to God's mercy, exhibiting his understanding of the necessity for atonement and the value of a right relationship with God.

Furthermore, the flood narrative presents a profound typology of salvation. Just as Noah and his family were saved from God's judgment by the ark, believers are saved from the ultimate judgment of sin by Jesus Christ. This analogy, drawn by the Apostle Peter, connects the waters of the flood with the waters of baptism, which symbolize not the removal of bodily dirt, but a good conscience towards God through the resurrection of Jesus Christ (1 Peter 3:20-21, ESV).

While the story of the Great Flood is a dramatic testament of God's power to judge sin, it is not devoid of grace and hope. God's righteousness and justice demand that sin be dealt with, and yet His love and mercy provide a way of escape from judgment. This juxtaposition of judgment and mercy in the flood narrative underscores the depth and breadth of God's character, serving as a poignant reminder of our responsibility to live righteously and seek His mercy.

2.2 The Destruction of Sodom and Gomorrah: Righteous Judgment

One of the most powerful instances of divine judgment in Scripture is seen in the destruction of Sodom and Gomorrah (Genesis 18:16-19:29, ASV). This narrative provides a stark revelation of God's righteousness, and yet, it is replete with the intricacies of divine mercy, human free will, and the dire consequences of unrepented sin.

Sodom and Gomorrah were cities renowned for their wickedness. God's impending judgment on them was disclosed to Abraham, whose nephew Lot lived in Sodom. The depth of the cities' depravity was such that the outcry against them had reached God's ears (Genesis 18:20, ASV).

Yet, before unleashing His judgment, God displayed His righteousness by discussing His intentions with Abraham, who interceded for the cities. This interaction presents a remarkable insight into the dialogue between divine foreknowledge and human free will. Abraham, utilizing his freedom, pleaded with God to spare the cities if righteous individuals were found within them, with the number eventually reduced to ten (Genesis 18:23-32, ASV). God agreed, indicating that His judgment was not arbitrary but depended on human actions, and that He was willing to withhold punishment if righteousness could be found.

However, the cities could not meet even this reduced threshold, underscoring the extent of their wickedness. Genesis 19:4-5 (ASV) paints a dark picture of Sodom's depravity when both young and old surrounded Lot's house, demanding to "know" the angelic visitors, a euphemism for sexual relations. Their behavior represented not only extreme sexual immorality but also a flagrant disregard for the sacred duties of hospitality.

In contrast, Lot's actions, though flawed and complex, reflect a sense of righteousness. He offered hospitality to the angels, and even attempted, regrettably, to offer his daughters to the mob in a misguided attempt to protect his guests (Genesis 19:6-8, ASV). His actions, while deeply problematic, indicated a willingness to uphold some moral codes, contrasting with the total depravity of the cities.

The angels intervened, struck the mob with blindness, and warned Lot to escape with his family as God was about to destroy the cities (Genesis 19:11-13, ASV). Here, divine judgment and mercy intersect. The same angels who brought the news of judgment also provided a way of escape, demonstrating God's mercy towards the righteous.

God destroyed Sodom and Gomorrah with brimstone and fire, a divine judgment that was both sudden and complete (Genesis 19:24-25, ASV). This destruction stands as a testimony to God's righteous judgment and a warning to all subsequent generations against embracing rampant wickedness.

Lot's wife, who looked back despite being warned, turned into a pillar of salt (Genesis 19:26, ASV). Her act underlines the dire consequences of disobedience and the longing for a sinful past, serving as a solemn reminder of the importance of complete obedience in the face of God's judgment.

The New Testament references this historical event as an example of divine judgment. Jesus used it as a warning for those who would face the Judgment Day unaware (Luke 17:28-30, ESV), while Peter cited it as an example of God's judgment on the ungodly and His rescue of the righteous (2 Peter 2:6-9, ESV). Jude also cited Sodom and Gomorrah as a warning against sexual immorality and perversion (Jude 1:7, ESV).

However, the narrative also presents a profound insight into God's righteous judgment. It is not arbitrary or capricious but comes in response to human choices and actions, and even in judgment, there is an aspect of mercy, as seen in the escape of Lot and his daughters.

While Sodom and Gomorrah are historical realities, they also serve as metaphors for societies that reject God's moral order. Their destruction symbolizes the inevitable end of all who defy God's law and spurn His mercy. At the same time, Lot's rescue offers hope, demonstrating that God distinguishes between the righteous and the wicked, even in times of general judgment.

God's righteous judgment, as exemplified in the destruction of Sodom and Gomorrah, therefore, is a powerful demonstration of His holiness and justice. It reinforces the serious consequences of sin while highlighting God's merciful provision for those who seek righteousness. This narrative offers an enduring lesson for humanity: God's judgment is certain, but so is His mercy for those who choose righteousness over wickedness.

2.3 Pharaoh's Downfall: A Display of God's Power

The narrative of Pharaoh's downfall in the book of Exodus is a robust illustration of God's righteous judgment and an exposition of His absolute power. The account begins in Exodus 1 (ASV) with the Israelites' growing population in Egypt, which caused unease among the Egyptians, leading to their oppression. By the time of Moses' birth, a new Pharaoh, who did not know Joseph or acknowledge his significant contributions to Egypt's prosperity, had ascended the throne (Exodus 1:8, ASV).

Moses' story, from his birth to his call and subsequent face-off with Pharaoh, is a tale of divine orchestration, demonstrating God's sovereign control over human affairs. When Moses returned to Egypt after his encounter with God at the burning bush, he was tasked with delivering God's command to Pharaoh: "Let my people go, that they may serve me" (Exodus 7:16, ASV).

Pharaoh's hardening heart, detailed throughout the Exodus narrative, underlines the seriousness of rebellion against God's commands. The Bible describes Pharaoh's heart as being "hardened" (Exodus 7:13, 22; 8:15, 19, 32; 9:7, 34, 35; ASV). This theme is recurrent, accentuating the obstinate nature of human sin and rebellion, which can lead to God confirming individuals in their self-chosen path of disobedience.

The ten plagues that befell Egypt (Exodus 7:14-12:30, ASV) were not random acts of wrath but targeted demonstrations of God's power. Each plague corresponded to an Egyptian deity, effectively deconstructing Egypt's religious system and revealing the supremacy of Yahweh over the so-called gods of Egypt. For example, the plague of darkness was a direct affront to Ra, the sun god.

Yet, throughout the plagues, there were moments of mercy. The pauses between the plagues offered Pharaoh opportunities to change his course. God's judgments are not designed to destroy but to lead the guilty to repentance. But if the warnings are disregarded, the ensuing judgment is certain and severe.

The final plague, the death of the firstborn, culminated in the institution of the Passover (Exodus 12:1-13, ASV), an enduring reminder of God's deliverance and judgment. The blood on the doorposts of the Israelite houses was a sign for the angel of death to "pass over" those homes, thus sparing them from the judgment befalling Egypt. It symbolized God's salvation for those under the blood covenant, underscoring the connection between deliverance and judgment.

After the tenth plague, Pharaoh finally released the Israelites, but not for long. He pursued them to the Red Sea, setting the stage for another grand demonstration of God's power – the parting of the Red Sea (Exodus 14:21-31, ASV). When the Egyptians attempted to cross, the sea returned to its place, drowning Pharaoh's army. The oppressive regime that had bound Israel for over four centuries was finally and decisively defeated.

The New Testament looks back at the Exodus event as an example of faith and judgment (Hebrews 11:29, ESV; 1 Corinthians 10:1-5, ESV). In Romans 9:17-18 (ESV), Paul cited Pharaoh's hardened heart as an example of God's sovereign right to show mercy or harden whom He wills, further affirming God's authority and absolute power in the face of human rebellion.

God's dealings with Pharaoh demonstrate His supreme power over the most powerful human authority of the time. This narrative, like the accounts of the flood and the destruction of Sodom and Gomorrah, offers a vivid reminder of God's ability to judge wickedness. But at the same time, it shows His willingness to spare and redeem those who heed His call and align with His purposes. This aspect of God's character is crucial to understanding His righteous judgment: it always carries the dual function of meting out justice and inviting repentance.

2.4 The Canaanite Conquest: God's Power in Action

The conquest of Canaan, as detailed in the book of Joshua, is a monumental testament to God's power in action. Not only did it signify the fulfillment of God's promise to Abraham that his descendants would inhabit the land (Genesis 12:7, ASV), but it also served as a display of God's judgment on the Canaanite nations.

The Canaanites' moral depravity is not to be underestimated. The inhabitants of Canaan were deeply immersed in practices that God had explicitly forbidden, such as idolatry, child sacrifice, incest, and various forms of sexual immorality (Leviticus 18:24-28, ASV). Their wickedness had reached a critical point where God's patience had been exhausted, and His judgment was now due.

The role of the Israelites in the conquest was not as conquerors, but as God's instruments of judgment. As Deuteronomy 9:4 (ASV) declares, it was not because of Israel's righteousness that they were going to possess the land, but because of the wickedness of these nations that the Lord was driving them out. The conquest was, therefore, an enactment of divine judgment, grounded in God's absolute righteousness and justice.

The battle of Jericho, the first major conflict in the conquest of Canaan, is a perfect example of God's power in action. Despite the formidable walls and fortifications of the city, the Israelites were able to conquer Jericho, not by their military prowess, but through their obedience to God's command (Joshua 6:2-5, ASV). God's miraculous intervention in causing the walls of Jericho to collapse demonstrated His ability to triumph over human defenses, rendering them futile before His power (Joshua 6:20, ASV).

God's power was also on full display in the battle against the Amorite kings, where He hurled large hailstones from heaven that killed more than the Israelites slew with the sword (Joshua 10:11, ASV). Moreover, at Joshua's request, God caused the sun to stand still, enabling the Israelites to finish the battle in a single day (Joshua 10:12-14, ASV). These extraordinary events were indisputable affirmations of God's power and His commitment to fulfilling His promises.

However, the conquest was not an unrestrained extermination. Rahab's story illustrates that there was still room for mercy. Rahab, a Canaanite prostitute, had heard of God's mighty acts and chose to align herself with Him. As a result, she and her family were spared during the destruction of Jericho (Joshua 2:1-21; 6:17, 22-25, ASV). Rahab's story underscores that God's judgment is never arbitrary or indiscriminate; there is always an opportunity for repentance and redemption for those who turn to Him.

The New Testament affirms that the events of the conquest were not only historical realities but also contained spiritual implications for God's people. The author of Hebrews cites Rahab's faith as a commendable example (Hebrews 11:31, ESV), and Paul points to the Israelites' experiences as warnings for Christians (1 Corinthians 10:1-11, ESV). The conquest of Canaan underscores the reality of God's judgment but also His patience, righteousness, and mercy.

In conclusion, the conquest of Canaan was a profound display of God's power in action. It was a testament to His judgment on the wicked and His faithfulness to His promises. This narrative serves as a sobering reminder that while God is patient and merciful, His patience does not equate to tolerance of sin. As God's people today, we are called to remember His righteous judgments and respond with reverence, obedience, and faith, knowing that the same power that delivered the Israelites is still at work among us today.

2.5 The Babylonian Exile: A Lesson in Humility

The Babylonian Exile, also known as the Babylonian Captivity, was one of the most significant events in the history of ancient Israel. Taking place in the 6th century B.C.E., it was a time marked by destruction, displacement, and profound loss. Yet, it was also a time of significant spiritual development, during which the people of Israel had to confront their unfaithfulness to God. It was a time of divine judgment, but also of divine instruction.

The exile was a direct result of Israel's persistent disobedience and idolatry. Despite the warnings of prophets like Isaiah and Jeremiah, the Israelites continually violated the covenant they had with God, engaging in practices such as idol worship and social injustice (Isaiah 1:4, 23; Jeremiah 22:13, ASV). Their actions brought about God's judgment, which came in the form of the Babylonian invasion. In 586 B.C.E., the Babylonian king Nebuchadnezzar besieged Jerusalem, destroyed the Temple, and took many Israelites into exile in Babylon (2 Kings 25:1-21, ASV).

This period was a painful but necessary lesson in humility for the Israelites. Stripped of their land, their Temple, and their independence, they were confronted with the harsh reality of their situation. They had ignored God's commandments, and now they were paying the price. Their pride and self-reliance had led them to this point of despair and humiliation.

Yet, even in the midst of this punishment, God's purpose was not merely to destroy but to correct and restore. The prophets, particularly Jeremiah and Ezekiel, provided the exiles with a divine perspective on their predicament. They stressed that the exile was not an accident or the result of mere political maneuvering, but God's deliberate act of judgment on their sin (Jeremiah 25:8-11, ASV).

However, God's intention was not to abandon His people permanently. The prophets also spoke of a time of restoration, emphasizing that the exile was not an end but a means to an end. God, through His prophet Jeremiah, promised that after seventy years, He would bring His people back to their land (Jeremiah 29:10-14, ASV).

In this way, the exile served as a time of spiritual reformation for Israel. Stripped of the distractions of their former life, the people were forced to consider their relationship with God seriously. They had to learn to rely on Him alone, recognizing their inability to save themselves. This period led to a revival of monotheism and a deeper commitment to the Torah among the Jewish people.

The Babylonian Exile has significant implications for our understanding of God's judgment and His character. First, it underscores the fact that God takes sin seriously. He is a God of justice who will not overlook transgressions indefinitely. Yet, He is also a God of mercy, willing to forgive and restore those who repent. He uses judgment, not to annihilate, but to correct, instruct, and bring about repentance.

Secondly, the exile highlights the role of human responsibility in the relationship with God. Despite His foreknowledge, God does not override human free will. He allows His people to experience the consequences of their actions to lead them to repentance.

Finally, the exile offers a poignant reminder that God's plans are not thwarted by human failure or external circumstances. Despite Israel's disobedience and the destruction of Jerusalem, God's promises remained. He was still able to bring about His purposes, demonstrating His sovereign power and faithfulness.

In conclusion, the Babylonian Exile was a dark period in Israel's history, marked by judgment and suffering. Yet, it was also a time of spiritual growth, demonstrating God's power to turn even the direst circumstances into opportunities for repentance and restoration. The exile serves as a stark reminder of God's judgment against sin, but also of His boundless mercy and faithfulness. It underscores the crucial importance of humility, repentance, and dependence on God, lessons that remain relevant for God's people today.

2.6 God's Judgment: A Call to Righteous Living

When considering God's judgment, it is essential to understand that His justice is a facet of His character, intricately tied to His love, mercy, and righteousness. Rather than interpreting divine judgment as merely punitive, it should be seen as a call to righteousness, a form of divine guidance pointing us towards the path of moral rectitude and spiritual flourishing.

God's judgment, throughout both the Old and New Testaments, stands as an unambiguous reminder of the importance of righteousness, an intrinsic adherence to the moral and ethical principles as delineated in God's commandments. The function of divine judgment is not purely retributive; it is fundamentally instructive and restorative, designed to bring about repentance, change, and ultimately, a deepened relationship with God.

Consider the case of ancient Israel. Despite God's repeated warnings through His prophets, the Israelites continually strayed from the path of righteousness, engaging in idol worship and acts of social injustice. Consequently, they experienced God's judgment in the form of Assyrian and Babylonian captivities (2 Kings 17:6-23; 25:8-21, ASV). Yet, these judgments were not arbitrary or vengeful. Rather, they served as a call to repentance and righteous living.

Similar themes of judgment as a call to righteousness permeate the New Testament. For instance, the Apostle Paul, in Romans 2:5 (ESV), warns that "because of your hard and impenitent heart you are storing up wrath for yourself on the day of wrath when God's righteous judgment will be revealed." However, this warning serves as a call to repentance and righteous living rather than a mere prediction of doom.

Moreover, the life, teachings, death, and resurrection of Jesus Christ present the most profound demonstration of God's judgment as a call to righteous living. Christ bore the weight of humanity's sin and underwent the ultimate judgment on our behalf. His sacrifice underscores the seriousness of sin and the depth of God's love and mercy, while simultaneously issuing a call to righteousness. As stated in Romans 6:4 (ESV), "We were buried therefore with him by baptism into death, in order that, just as Christ was raised from the dead by the glory of the Father, we too might walk in newness of life."

God's judgments, therefore, serve as a severe yet loving call to align our lives with His moral standards. It's a call to recognize our limitations, failures, and need for divine mercy and grace. The call to righteousness is not merely an external adherence to religious laws; rather, it is an inward transformation resulting in a lifestyle that reflects God's character.

However, this call does not negate human free will. God, in His foreknowledge, knows the decisions individuals will freely make. Nevertheless, this foreknowledge doesn't compromise or dictate human free will. Consequently, each person has the personal responsibility to respond to God's call to righteousness. This responsibility highlights the importance of understanding and applying the Bible's teachings accurately and in a balanced manner, which in turn influences our choices and actions.

The importance of righteous living is further highlighted in our prayer life. God is not a "slot machine," dispensing answers according to our whims. He responds to prayers aligned with His will and righteousness. Our prayers, therefore, should reflect our commitment to righteousness and our willingness to align our lives with His purposes.

In conclusion, understanding God's judgment as a call to righteous living helps us view divine justice within the context of God's overarching love, mercy, and righteousness. It underscores the importance of personal responsibility, humility, and continuous spiritual growth.

Chapter 3: The Almighty Shield: God's Power to Protect

3.1 The Exodus: A Mighty Display of Protection

One of the most illustrative examples of God's power to protect is the Exodus event when God, in His faithfulness, freed the Israelites from the bondage of Egypt. The Exodus event isn't just a singular act of deliverance; it is a rich tapestry of miracles and manifestations of God's power, foreknowledge, and commitment to protecting His chosen people.

God's Foreknowledge and Protection

When the story begins, we find the Israelites suffering under the oppressive rule of a Pharaoh who did not know Joseph (Exodus 1:8, ASV). God, in His foreknowledge, was aware of the suffering of His people. He heard their groaning and remembered His covenant with Abraham, Isaac, and Jacob (Exodus 2:24, ASV). God's foreknowledge does not compromise human free will, but His intervention often occurs when His people call out to Him in their distress.

The Burning Bush: The Call of Moses

The divine intervention began with the calling of Moses, a man chosen by God to lead His people out of Egypt. Moses, while tending his father-in-law's flock, encountered God in a burning bush, an event that would forever alter the course of his life (Exodus 3:1-10, ASV).

God said to Moses, "I have surely seen the affliction of my people that are in Egypt and have heard their cry by reason of their taskmasters; for I know their sorrows" (Exodus 3:7, ASV). This shows that God, while timeless and omniscient, is intimately concerned with the sufferings of His people and has a plan to protect and deliver them.

Signs and Wonders: Display of God's Power

God demonstrated His power through signs and wonders, which served both as judgment against Egypt and as proof of His divine protection over Israel. The ten plagues were not arbitrary acts of violence but a direct challenge to the false gods of Egypt. Each plague represented God's authority over the deities the Egyptians worshipped and showed the Israelites that their God was more powerful than their oppressors' gods.

For instance, the plague of darkness, a total blackout that lasted for three days, was a direct affront to Ra, the sun god of Egypt (Exodus 10:21-23, ASV). In this impenetrable darkness, God provided light in the dwellings of the Israelites, an overt sign of His protective power.

The Passover: The Definitive Act of Protection

The final plague, the death of the firstborn, culminated in the establishment of the Passover, an everlasting ordinance for the Israelites (Exodus 12:14, ASV). God instructed the Israelites to mark their doorposts with the blood of a sacrificed lamb, and when God saw the blood, He would "pass over" that house, sparing those inside from the destructive plague (Exodus 12:23, ASV). The blood of the lamb served as a protective sign against divine judgment.

The Exodus: Journey to Freedom

Following the ten plagues, Pharaoh finally released the Israelites, and they began their journey to freedom. At the Red Sea, God delivered the Israelites in a spectacular fashion, parting the waters so that they could cross on dry ground. When the Egyptians pursued, God caused the sea to return, drowning their entire army (Exodus 14:21-28, ASV). This miraculous event underscored God's protection, ensuring the survival and freedom of His people.

God's Ongoing Protection in the Wilderness

Even after the Exodus, God's protective care continued during the Israelites' wilderness journey. He provided manna and quail for their sustenance (Exodus 16:13-15, ASV), ensured their safety, and led them with a pillar of cloud by day and a pillar of fire by night (Exodus 13:21, ASV).

Conclusion: Protection Calls for Faithful Obedience

The Exodus narrative underscores God's unwavering commitment to protect His people, demonstrating His might and supremacy over all earthly powers. However, it also underscores the reciprocal commitment that God's people must have. God's protective power does not negate the need for faithful obedience.

God's protection, manifested powerfully in the Exodus, continues today. However, it is essential to remember that God's protection doesn't mean the absence of trials or suffering. Instead, it assures us of His presence and help in the midst of adversity, guiding us towards righteousness.

In the grand narrative of Scripture, God's power to protect isn't an insurance policy against all hardship. Instead, it's a divine assurance that in our journey of faith, amidst trials and tribulations, God is with us, guiding, providing for, and protecting us, urging us toward a life of faith, obedience, and righteousness. Just as the Israelites learned to trust God's guidance in the wilderness, so too are Christians called to trust in God's protective power in their journey towards the Promised Land of eternal life through Jesus Christ.

God's power to protect is not just a historical reality but an ongoing promise to all who will put their trust in Him. The Exodus story serves as a timeless reminder that the God who shielded His people from the plagues, parted the Red Sea, and led them through the wilderness, continues to protect His people today. His faithfulness endures forever, and His power to protect remains undiminished.

3.2 Daniel in the Lion's Den: Unseen Shields

The narrative of Daniel in the lion's den provides a profound illustration of God's power to protect His servants, even in the face of seemingly insurmountable danger. It is a testament to the unseen shields that God places around those who remain steadfast in their faith and obedience.

Setting the Stage: Daniel's Exemplary Faithfulness

As we explore this iconic Biblical narrative, it's crucial to understand the character of Daniel. He was taken captive from Jerusalem and served under several rulers in Babylon. Yet, despite the challenges and cultural pressures, Daniel consistently demonstrated faithfulness to God and commitment to righteousness.

Daniel was an exceptional administrator, which garnered him favor with King Darius, who planned to set him over the entire kingdom (Daniel 6:3, ASV). Daniel's faithfulness to God, which led to his professional excellence, ironically set the stage for the perilous situation that would follow.

Plot Against Daniel: The Test of Faith

Jealous of Daniel's favor with the king, other administrators and satraps plotted against him. Knowing his unwavering faith, they manipulated King Darius into issuing an irrevocable decree that, for thirty days, anyone who petitioned any god or man other than Darius would be cast into the lion's den (Daniel 6:7, ASV).

Despite the decree, Daniel continued his regular practice of praying to God three times a day, with his windows open towards Jerusalem (Daniel 6:10, ASV). This defiance was not a reckless or prideful act but a manifestation of his steadfast faith in God.

Into the Lion's Den: God's Protection Manifests

Upon learning of Daniel's continued prayers, the king, bound by the laws of the Medes and Persians, reluctantly ordered Daniel to be thrown into the lion's den. However, Darius expressed hope in Daniel's God to rescue him, highlighting Daniel's influence and the reputation of his God (Daniel 6:16, ASV).

Overnight, Daniel remained in the den of hungry lions. Yet, when King Darius came at dawn, Daniel was found unharmed. Daniel declared, "My God hath sent his angel, and hath shut the lions' mouths, and they have not hurt me; forasmuch as before him innocency was found in me; and also before thee, O king, have I done no hurt" (Daniel 6:22, ASV).

This narrative confirms the fact that God's protection isn't an insurance policy against trials but rather a reassurance of His presence in times of adversity. Even in the direst circumstances, God's protective shield is fully active, preserving those who love Him and walk according to His commands.

The Unseen Shield: God's Angelic Protection

The presence of God's angel in the lion's den signifies God's unseen shields, often manifesting in ways beyond our understanding. In the midst of the seemingly impossible situation, God's divine intervention superseded the laws of nature, leaving the mighty lions powerless against Daniel.

This instance is not an isolated event; it aligns with many other biblical accounts wherein God used angels as protective shields (Psalm 91:11-12; Hebrews 1:14, ESV). Such divine protection doesn't remove us from the face of danger; instead, it ensures we are not consumed by it, demonstrating God's sovereignty even over the most ferocious beasts.

The Outcome: God's Protection as Testimony

The deliverance of Daniel had a far-reaching impact. King Darius issued a decree that in his entire kingdom, people must fear and reverence Daniel's God, "for he is the living God, enduring forever; his kingdom shall never be destroyed, and his dominion shall be to the end" (Daniel 6:26, ESV).

Conclusion: Unseen Shields in Our Lives

The story of Daniel in the lion's den is a profound reminder of God's power to protect. The invisible shield that God placed around Daniel is available to all who remain faithful to God, and such protection often goes beyond our comprehension.

God's protection doesn't mean we will never face adversity or hardship. But, as we remain faithful to God and walk in obedience to His commands, we can have confidence that the same God who shut the mouths of the lions for Daniel oversees our lives. We may not always see or understand His methods, but we can trust in His faithfulness and unfailing power to protect.

In our lives, we may encounter metaphorical "lion's dens"—situations that threaten to consume us. But Daniel's story assures us that even there, God's protective power is at work. Our responsibility is to remain faithful, trusting in God's protection, and His power to turn even the most threatening situations into testimonies of His faithfulness. This unseen shield of God's protection is a testament to His love, a reassurance that "He who dwells in the shelter of the Most High will abide in the shadow of the Almighty" (Psalm 91:1, ESV).

3.3 The Preservation of the Remnant: God's Protective Hand

The concept of a "remnant" in the Bible signifies the faithful few who endure amidst widespread unfaithfulness. The preservation of this remnant, particularly in the Old Testament, demonstrates the protective hand of God even in times of widespread judgment, showcasing His mercy, justice, and providence.

The Concept of the Remnant: Faith Amid Unfaithfulness

The term "remnant" often refers to the survivors of a catastrophe or those who remain faithful to God amidst the spiritual decline of their people. In essence, it represents a minority who uphold God's commands and seek His will, regardless of the broader societal or religious context (Isaiah 10:20-22, ASV).

Preservation during the Flood: Noah's Family

One of the earliest examples of God's preservation of the remnant is the account of Noah and the Flood. Amidst a world steeped in wickedness, Noah found grace in the eyes of God because he was "righteous and blameless in his generation and walked with God" (Genesis 6:9, ASV).

God's protection of Noah and his family from the global flood is indicative of His commitment to preserve the righteous, even during widespread judgment. In this scenario, God's protective hand shielded the remnant (Noah's family), preserving humanity and demonstrating His mercy.

Preservation during the Babylonian Exile: A Faithful Remnant

Another potent example of God's preservation of the remnant is evident during the Babylonian exile. Israel had descended into rampant idolatry, leading to their eventual captivity by Babylon as divine punishment.

Despite the seeming obliteration of the nation, God preserved a remnant. For example, Daniel, Shadrach, Meshach, and Abednego were part of this faithful remnant in Babylon, serving God unwaveringly in a foreign land (Daniel 1:6-20, ASV). They embody

God's promise in 2 Chronicles 7:14 (ASV): "if my people, who are called by my name, shall humble themselves, and pray, and seek my face, and turn from their wicked ways; then will I hear from heaven, and will forgive their sin, and will heal their land."

God's hand of protection over His faithful remnant amidst the Babylonian captivity illustrates His providence and commitment to His covenant. The returned exiles (Ezra 9:13-15, ASV) highlight this preservation, emphasizing that God never abandons His people, even during severe judgment.

The Remnant in the New Testament: Spiritual Israel

In the New Testament, the concept of the remnant extends to "spiritual Israel"—those, whether Jew or Gentile, who accept Christ as their Savior. In Romans 9:27, Paul quotes Isaiah, underscoring that although Israelites may be as numerous as the sand by the sea, only a remnant will be saved (Romans 9:27, ESV).

God's preservation of this spiritual remnant, made evident through the death and resurrection of Jesus Christ, amplifies His divine protective hand. Believers are sealed with the promised Holy Spirit, who is the guarantee of our inheritance until we acquire possession of it (Ephesians 1:13-14, ESV). This points to God's eternal protection over His faithful remnant, offering assurance of divine preservation, both now and for eternity.

Conclusion: God's Protective Hand Today

God's preservation of the remnant throughout biblical history is not merely a historical observation but a living promise for today's believers. In an era of moral decline and societal unrest, those who stand firm in their faith, adhering to God's Word, are the remnant—under the protective shield of the Almighty.

Regardless of the trials or tribulations we face, God's protective hand remains over His people. Like Noah, we find grace in God's sight by walking with Him. Like Daniel and his companions, we maintain our faith in foreign lands, and like the first-century believers, we hold onto the hope of our salvation in Christ.

This understanding of God's protective hand over the remnant reassures believers of His unchanging nature. God's providence over the remnant reveals His heart—merciful, just, and protective. It should inspire us to persevere in faith, fully assured that the God who preserved the remnant in biblical times continues to do so today, wrapping His faithful believers with an eternal shield of divine protection.

3.4 God's Power in Spiritual Warfare

The concept of spiritual warfare permeates both the Old and New Testaments. As Christians, we're engaged in a battle not against flesh and blood, but against spiritual forces (Ephesians 6:12, ESV). Recognizing God's power in spiritual warfare is crucial for understanding His protective role in our lives.

The Battle is the Lord's: Old Testament Insights

In the Old Testament, God's power in spiritual warfare is displayed vividly. For instance, the Israelites, under Joshua's leadership, saw God's power as they faced insurmountable odds. They were instructed to march around Jericho, blowing trumpets and shouting, and God delivered the city into their hands (Joshua 6:1-20, ASV).

This example reinforces that the battle belongs to the Lord (1 Samuel 17:47, ASV). In spiritual warfare, our might or strategies aren't what win the battle; rather, it is God's power that overcomes. We participate in the battle, but it is God's divine intervention that ensures victory.

Armor of God: New Testament Teachings

The New Testament provides a more explicit description of spiritual warfare and God's power therein. In Ephesians 6:10-18, Paul describes the full armor of God, emphasizing the believer's need to rely on God's power in the spiritual battle. The components of this armor—the belt of truth, the breastplate of righteousness, the shoes of the gospel of peace, the shield of faith, the helmet of salvation, and the sword of the Spirit—all point to God's provisions for spiritual warfare.

Each piece of the armor symbolizes a critical aspect of the Christian faith, reinforcing the truth that our power comes from God alone. For instance, the "sword of the Spirit" is described as the word of God, suggesting that understanding and applying Scripture correctly is essential for spiritual victory (Ephesians 6:17, ESV).

God's Protective Power: Divine Defense and Offense

Recognizing God's power in spiritual warfare also involves understanding His role in both defense and offense. The components of the armor of God serve defensive functions—providing protection from attacks of the enemy, while the "sword of the Spirit" and prayer provide means for offensive action.

God protects us by giving us truth to counteract lies, righteousness to withstand accusations, readiness to spread peace instead of discord, faith to deflect fiery darts of doubt, salvation to guard our minds, and His Word to combat falsehoods. Simultaneously, He equips us to advance His kingdom through His Word and prayer.

The Ultimate Victory: Christ's Triumph

The New Testament underscores that the ultimate victory in spiritual warfare has been achieved through Jesus Christ. His death and resurrection have defeated sin and death, securing victory for all who believe in Him (1 Corinthians 15:57, ESV). This doesn't mean that we won't face spiritual battles—indeed, Peter warns us to be alert to the devil's schemes (1 Peter 5:8, ESV)—but it reassures us that the outcome of the war has been decisively determined.

Conclusion: Relying on God's Power

God's power in spiritual warfare is an essential part of His protective character. It reassures us that no matter what spiritual battles we face, we can rely on His power. The onus is on us to put on the full armor of God daily, apply His Word accurately in our lives, and trust in His ultimate victory. As we do this, we can experience God's power and protection, even in the midst of spiritual warfare. This power is not a miraculous indwelling force that guides us, but it is realized as we apply God's inspired words correctly in our lives, ensuring our spiritual survival and growth.

3.5 Our Refuge and Strength: Personal Experiences of God's Protection

Throughout the pages of the Bible and across the spectrum of human experience, God's protection remains a powerful theme. Our journey through the scripture has illustrated how God's power protects His people from physical harm, preserves a remnant, and guards us in spiritual warfare. However, God's protection also extends into the individual, personal realm of our lives. As we navigate life's challenges, we repeatedly discover that God is our refuge and strength, a very present help in trouble (Psalm 46:1, ASV).

Job: A Testament to God's Protection Amid Suffering

Job, an upright man who feared God, experienced profound personal suffering (Job 1:1, ASV). He lost his wealth, his children, and his health, seemingly without reason. Yet even in the face of intense trials, Job experienced God's protection.

This protection did not take the form of physical preservation from hardship. Instead, God shielded Job's faith, allowing him to maintain his integrity and remain steadfast in his trust in God (Job 2:9-10, ASV). Job's story demonstrates that God's protection might not always shield us from trials, but it can preserve our faith, leading us to a deeper understanding of God's sovereignty and goodness.

Paul: God's Power Made Perfect in Weakness

In the New Testament, the Apostle Paul offers another personal testimony of God's protection. After being given a "thorn in the flesh," Paul pleaded with the Lord to remove it. Instead of removing the thorn, however, God responded, "My grace is sufficient for you, for my power is made perfect in weakness" (2 Corinthians 12:7-9, ESV).

God's protective power was evident not by removing the trial, but by giving Paul the grace to endure and by using Paul's weakness to display divine strength. Paul's experience reminds us that God's protection does not always equate to the absence of struggle. Instead, it can manifest in the strength to endure hardship and the grace to glorify God within it.

God's Protection in Our Lives: A Personal Encounter

Much like Job and Paul, we can see God's protective power at work in our personal lives. This is not to say we will be free from trials or hardship. Instead, God's protection often means that despite life's storms, we can find peace, strength, and refuge in Him.

When we face financial difficulties, God's protection may not necessarily mean a sudden inflow of wealth, but the provision of our needs and the wisdom to handle resources wisely (Philippians 4:19, ESV). In illness, it might not always mean immediate healing, but the strength to endure, a peace that transcends understanding, and, sometimes, physical recovery (Philippians 4:7, ESV). In the face of conflict, it might mean not the absence of opposition but the grace to respond in love and the wisdom to pursue peace (Romans 12:18-21, ESV).

God's Protection and Human Responsibility

Recognizing God's protection does not absolve us of responsibility. Proverbs contains many instructions about living wisely, indicating that while God is our protector, we should also make wise, godly decisions (Proverbs 2:1-11, ASV). This includes everything from our financial choices to how we respond to potential health issues. Our actions can either align with God's protective intent or disregard it.

Conclusion: God Our Protector

God's protection is more than a divine force field that shields us from all harm. It's the assurance that in every situation, He is with us, providing strength, wisdom, and refuge. It's the knowledge that no matter how fierce the storm, we are secure in Him. Our faith, grounded in the Holy Spirit-inspired Word of God, remains our steadfast shield, and our actions, when aligned with this faith, attest to God's protective power in our lives.

As we experience God's protection personally, we learn to trust Him more deeply and recognize His work more readily. And as we share our experiences with others, we spread the assurance that our God is indeed a refuge and strength, the almighty shield whose power protects each of His children.

3.6 The Ultimate Protection: The Promise of Eternal Life

The ultimate manifestation of God's protective power is His promise of eternal life to those who trust in Jesus Christ. The journey through this life can be riddled with challenges, sorrows, and afflictions. Yet, for the faithful believer, these trials are but transient shadows preceding the brilliant dawn of eternity. God, in His infinite love and power, offers us protection that transcends the temporal and enters the realm of the eternal.

The Promise of Eternal Life in the Old Testament

Even in the Old Testament, before the coming of Christ, the promise of life beyond death is hinted at. In the book of Job, for example, despite his extreme suffering, Job expresses his belief in life beyond the grave: "I know that my Redeemer lives, and at the last he will stand upon the earth. And after my skin has been thus destroyed, yet in my flesh, I shall see God" (Job 19:25-26, ASV). In the midst of his trials, Job clings to this hope, a testimony to the ultimate protection God provides: the hope of life eternal.

The Promise of Eternal Life in the New Testament

With the advent of Christ, the promise of eternal life becomes even clearer. Jesus Himself declares, "For God so loved the world, that he gave his only Son, that whoever believes in him should not perish but have eternal life" (John 3:16, ESV). This is the heart of the Gospel message: through faith in Jesus Christ, we are granted eternal life, offering us ultimate protection from the power of sin and death.

The Nature of Eternal Life

Eternal life, as presented in the Bible, is not merely an extension of our earthly existence. It represents a profound transformation of our being and circumstances. We will be changed "in a moment, in the twinkling of an eye, at the last trumpet. For the trumpet will sound, and the dead will be raised imperishable, and we shall be changed" (1 Corinthians 15:52, ESV). In eternity, our mortal, sinful selves will be transformed into imperishable, sinless beings.

Furthermore, eternal life means living in the presence of God. Revelation gives us a glimpse of this reality: "He will wipe away every tear from their eyes, and death shall be no more, neither shall there be mourning, nor crying, nor pain anymore, for the former things have passed away" (Revelation 21:4, ESV). The protection of eternal life encompasses not just our bodies, but also our minds and souls, providing complete relief from sorrow, pain, and death.

Eternal Life: A Gift, Not a Right

It's vital to understand that eternal life is not something we earn or deserve. It's a gift from God, given out of His love and grace. Ephesians states clearly, "For by grace you have been saved through faith. And this is not your own doing; it is the gift of God, not a result of works, so that no one may boast" (Ephesians 2:8-9, ESV). We cannot work our way into eternal life; it's a divine gift, the ultimate expression of God's protective love.

Living in the Light of Eternal Life

The promise of eternal life should shape our lives here and now. First, it gives us a living hope that inspires us to persevere, even in the face of trials and tribulations. Second, it motivates us to live righteously, knowing that our actions here on earth have eternal implications. Lastly, it compels us to share this great hope with others, extending God's protection to all who would receive it.

God's power to protect manifests in many ways: from the preservation of the remnant, through spiritual warfare, in personal experiences of His providence, to the ultimate protection – the promise of eternal life. This eternal life is our shield against despair, our comfort in affliction, our hope amidst uncertainty, and our assurance of God's unwavering, protective love. It's a gift, freely given by our loving God to those who put their faith in Jesus Christ.

While we navigate life's storms, may we keep our eyes fixed on this heavenly promise. For the believer, the trials of this life are fleeting, a temporary sojourn before we reach our eternal home. God, our almighty shield, not only navigates us through life's tempests but also secures for us a future where "He will wipe away every tear from their eyes, and death shall be no more" (Revelation 21:4, ESV). Such is the ultimate protection God provides, a promise of life everlasting in His divine presence.

Chapter 4: Redeemed: God's Power to Restore

4.1 The Prodigal Son: A Parable of Restoration

One of the most compelling parables Jesus told is the story of the Prodigal Son (Luke 15:11-32, ESV). It's a tale that vividly illustrates God's power to restore even those who have fallen the furthest. This chapter delves into the profound lessons this parable provides on the nature of sin, repentance, forgiveness, and divine restoration.

The Narrative

The narrative begins with a younger son who audaciously asks his father for his share of the inheritance – an act tantamount to wishing the father dead. The father grants his request, and the younger son goes to a distant land, where he squanders his wealth in reckless living.

When a severe famine hits the land, the son is reduced to feeding pigs, an unclean animal in Jewish custom, and he longs to fill his belly with the pods the pigs eat – a symbol of utter degradation. This is the turning point in the story, where the younger son "came to himself" (Luke 15:17, ESV), recognizing his folly and the need to return home.

On his return, the father sees him from afar and, filled with compassion, runs to his son, embraces him, and calls for a feast to celebrate his return. It's a moment of profound grace and unconditional love, embodying the essence of divine restoration.

Sin and Separation

The younger son's request for his inheritance and his subsequent actions reflect the nature of sin. Sin, like the son's request, is a demand for autonomy from God, a desire to live one's life apart from His guidance and authority. It's a choice that leads to spiritual separation, symbolized by the son's journey to a distant land.

Yet, sin's pleasures are fleeting, and its consequences are severe. The younger son, having squandered his wealth, ends up in a state of destitution, illustrating the wages of sin. It brings momentary pleasure, but ultimately leads to spiritual, emotional, and even physical ruin.

Repentance and Return

The turning point in the son's journey is a moment of profound self-realization. The younger son recognizes his dire situation and admits his guilt: "I have sinned against heaven and before you" (Luke 15:18, ESV). This confession represents true repentance – an acknowledgment of one's sin and a decision to turn back to God.

Repentance is not merely feeling sorry for the consequences of sin. It's a change of heart, a decision to leave behind the path of disobedience and return to God's embrace. It's the first crucial step towards divine restoration.

Forgiveness and Restoration

The father's reaction to his son's return is a potent picture of God's grace. Instead of retribution or rejection, the father offers forgiveness and acceptance. He orders his servants to bring the best robe, put a ring on his son's hand, and sandals on his feet, and to kill the fattened calf for a celebratory feast.

Each of these elements symbolizes restoration. The best robe signifies honor and dignity, the ring authority and sonship, the sandals denote freedom (as opposed to the bare feet of slaves), and the feast represents joy and celebration. The father's actions illuminate the depths of God's redemptive love and His power to restore the repentant sinner to a state of honor, authority, freedom, and joy.

The Older Son and Self-Righteousness

The parable also cautions against self-righteousness, personified by the older son. He resents the father's grace towards his errant brother and refuses to join the celebration. His indignation reveals a lack of understanding of his father's love and a failure to rejoice in his brother's restoration. It's a warning against the self-righteous attitude that begrudges God's grace towards repentant sinners, reminding us that all need grace and none can claim superiority based on self-righteousness.

The parable of the Prodigal Son vividly illustrates God's power to restore. It underscores that no one is too far gone for God's redemption, that genuine repentance leads to divine forgiveness, and that God's restoration is complete and joyous. However, it also warns against the dangers of self-righteousness and calls for a humble recognition of our need for grace. Above all, it celebrates the beauty of divine restoration – a reflection of the redemptive love at the heart of the Gospel.

4.2 Job's Restoration: Triumph Over Trials

The narrative of Job is one of the most challenging and poignant accounts in the Old Testament, presenting a vivid portrayal of human suffering and divine sovereignty. Job's story, situated between tragedy and restoration, offers deep insights into the nature of trials and God's power to restore in the midst of profound pain.

The Onset of Job's Trials

Job was a man described as "blameless and upright, one who feared God and turned away from evil" (Job 1:1, ESV). He was richly blessed with prosperity and a large family. However, his life took a sudden turn when Satan, with God's permission, assailed him with catastrophic loss and severe physical affliction.

The question arises, why would God allow such suffering to befall a righteous man? This question is central to the book of Job and indeed, to the problem of evil and suffering in our world. However, while the text does not provide a direct answer, it highlights God's sovereignty, even in times of inexplicable suffering. It affirms that God's ways, though often unfathomable to us, are always rooted in His unchanging character of righteousness and love.

Job's Response to His Trials

Despite his profound suffering, Job initially responded with faith and resignation to God's sovereign will: "The Lord gave, and the Lord has taken away; blessed be the name of the Lord" (Job 1:21, ESV). Yet, as his trials persisted, Job descended into despair, questioning the fairness of his suffering and demanding an explanation from God.

Job's friends, believing his trials were divine punishment for hidden sin, insisted he repent. Yet, Job maintained his innocence. His lamentations, often stark and poignant, lay bare the depths of his anguish, inviting us to grapple with the raw honesty of his pain.

God's Answer and Job's Restoration

God's response to Job came not in the form of direct answers to his questions, but in a revelation of His divine nature and sovereign power (Job 38-41). This humbling encounter led Job to a deeper understanding of God, prompting his repentance for his presumptuous words: "I had heard of you by the hearing of the ear, but now my eye sees you; therefore I despise myself, and repent in dust and ashes" (Job 42:5-6, ESV).

Following this, God restored Job's fortunes, giving him twice as much as he had before. Job was blessed with a new family and lived to a ripe old age, experiencing God's favor and blessings (Job 42:10-17).

Lessons from Job's Trials and Restoration

Job's story offers several profound insights. First, it challenges the retribution principle – the idea that prosperity is a reward for righteousness, and suffering is a punishment for sin. Job's trials were not due to any wrong he had committed, affirming that suffering can be complex and not always a direct result of personal sin.

Second, it underscores that true faith trusts in God's character and sovereignty, even in the face of severe trials and unanswered questions. Job's journey was not a linear path from suffering to restoration but involved wrestling with doubt, despair, and the mystery of divine providence. Yet, it ultimately led to a deeper faith, rooted not in external blessings but in a personal encounter with God.

Finally, Job's restoration underscores that while God's deliverance might not always align with our expectations or timing, His plans for us are grounded in His infinite wisdom and steadfast love. His power to restore transcends our deepest pains and most profound losses, offering hope, healing, and wholeness.

In conclusion, Job's narrative of suffering and restoration provides a rich theological exploration of the problem of human suffering within the framework of divine sovereignty. It invites us to wrestle with profound questions, affirming that God's power to restore remains unwavering, even amidst the most intense trials. It reassures us that in the divine economy, no experience of pain is wasted but can lead to a deeper encounter with God, deeper faith, and ultimately, to divine restoration.

4.3 The Resurrection of Lazarus: A Glimpse of Restorative Power

One of the most vivid and profound demonstrations of God's restorative power in the New Testament is the resurrection of Lazarus, as recounted in John 11:1-44. This event not only affirmed Jesus' identity as the resurrection and the life but also provided a profound glimpse into God's power to restore life from death.

The Setting of the Miracle

At the beginning of the narrative, we learn that Lazarus, the brother of Mary and Martha, was sick. Despite the sisters' urgent message to Jesus, He delayed His arrival, stating, "This illness does not lead to death. It is for the glory of God, so that the Son of God may be glorified through it" (John 11:4, ESV). When Jesus finally decided to go to Bethany, Lazarus had been in the tomb for four days.

Jesus, the Resurrection and the Life

Upon His arrival, Jesus was met with deep grief from Mary, Martha, and the Jews who had come to mourn with them. Martha, expressing both disappointment and faith, said to Jesus, "Lord, if you had been here, my brother would not have died. But even now I know that whatever you ask from God, God will give you" (John 11:21-22, ESV).

Jesus responded with a profound declaration, "I am the resurrection and the life. Whoever believes in me, though he die, yet shall he live, and everyone who lives and believes in me shall never die. Do you believe this?" (John 11:25-26, ESV). This statement reveals Jesus as the source of eternal life, power over death, and ultimate restoration.

The Miracle of Resurrection

Despite the incredulity of some and the stench of death, Jesus commanded that the stone be removed from the entrance of the tomb. Then, Jesus prayed aloud to His Father, and with a loud voice, commanded Lazarus to come out. In an incredible display of divine power, Lazarus came out of the tomb, bound in his grave clothes, but alive.

Implications of Lazarus' Resurrection

The resurrection of Lazarus holds profound theological and practical implications. Firstly, it validates Jesus' identity as the Son of

God, the resurrection, and the life. It affirms His power over death, foreshadowing His own resurrection and the promise of eternal life for those who believe in Him.

Secondly, it reveals God's sovereignty and perfect timing. Jesus' deliberate delay demonstrates that God's ways and timing, though often perplexing from our limited perspective, are always perfect. It reminds us that even when God seems silent or distant in our trials, He is actively working for His glory and our ultimate good.

Finally, it provides a vivid glimpse of God's restorative power. Just as Jesus restored physical life to Lazarus, He can breathe spiritual life into our spiritually dead hearts, restoring our relationship with God and giving us the promise of eternal life.

This miracle encourages us that no situation is beyond the restorative power of Jesus. As He breathed life back into Lazarus, He can also breathe life into our dead situations, hopes, and dreams. The resurrection of Lazarus is a powerful illustration of the hope we have in Jesus, a reminder that in Him, death does not have the last word. Whether it be physical death, spiritual deadness, or the death of dreams and hopes, Jesus, the resurrection and the life, has the power to bring restoration and life.

The story of Lazarus is more than just an event; it is a promise, a declaration of hope for everyone. It is a promise that death is not the end, that we have a Savior who has power over death and can restore us to life. It is a declaration of hope, that even in our darkest moments, even when all seems lost, God can still bring restoration. It is an invitation to each of us, regardless of where we are in our lives, to come to Jesus, the resurrection and the life, for He alone can provide ultimate restoration and life.

4.4 Spiritual Restoration: From Death to Life

Spiritual restoration is a significant theme in the Bible, permeating both the Old and New Testaments. It represents the process of being restored to a right relationship with God, a transition from spiritual death to life, largely made possible through the sacrificial work of Jesus Christ on the cross.

The Reality of Spiritual Death

To grasp the significance of spiritual restoration, we must first understand the reality of spiritual death. According to Scripture, spiritual death is the state of being separated from God because of sin. "For the wages of sin is death" (Romans 6:23, ESV). Adam and Eve's disobedience in the Garden of Eden marked humanity's fall into sin, which resulted in both physical and spiritual death (Genesis 2:17).

In Ephesians 2:1-3, Paul further elaborates on our spiritual state before Christ: "And you were dead in the trespasses and sins in which you once walked" (ESV). Spiritual death is the default condition of every human being because of our sinful nature. It is a state of alienation from God, where we are unable to please Him or live according to His standards.

The Promise of Spiritual Life

Despite this grim reality, the story does not end there. God, in His great love and mercy, provided a way for spiritual restoration. God made a promise in the Old Testament through the prophet Ezekiel, "And I will give you a new heart, and a new spirit I will put within you. And I will remove the heart of stone from your flesh and give you a heart of flesh" (Ezekiel 36:26, ESV). This promise pointed to a future time of spiritual renewal and restoration.

The fulfillment of this promise is found in Jesus Christ. He came to earth to die on the cross, taking the penalty for our sins upon Himself, so that through faith in Him, we could be restored to a right relationship with God. As Paul wrote, "But God, being rich in mercy, because of the great love with which he loved us, even when we were dead in our trespasses, made us alive together with Christ—by grace you have been saved" (Ephesians 2:4-5, ESV). Through Christ, spiritual death is overcome, and spiritual life is granted.

Living in Spiritual Restoration

Being spiritually restored doesn't merely mean escaping the penalty of sin. It also involves a transformation of life. The Holy Spirit works in the believer's heart, enabling them to resist sin and live according to God's commands. This transformation process is often referred to as sanctification.

Paul writes in Romans 6:4, "We were therefore buried with him through baptism into death in order that, just as Christ was raised from the dead through the glory of the Father, we too may live a new life" (ESV). This new life is characterized by obedience to God, love for others, and the fruit of the Spirit (Galatians 5:22-23). It is a life that, while not free from struggles and trials, is marked by hope, peace, and joy that come from being in a right relationship with God.

The Hope of Eternal Life

The ultimate hope of spiritual restoration is eternal life. Jesus said, "For God so loved the world, that he gave his only Son, that whoever believes in him should not perish but have eternal life" (John 3:16, ESV). Those who are spiritually restored are given the promise of eternal life, a life that continues even after physical death. This eternal life is not merely an endless existence but a life of perfect communion with God, free from sin and sorrow.

In Revelation 21:4 (ESV), we catch a glimpse of what this eternal life looks like, "He will wipe away every tear from their eyes, and death shall be no more, neither shall there be mourning, nor crying, nor pain anymore, for the former things have passed away." In this future restored state, we will experience the fullness of God's redemptive work.

In conclusion, spiritual restoration is a powerful aspect of God's redemptive plan. It is the process of moving from spiritual death—alienation and separation from God due to sin—to spiritual life—reconciliation and union with God through the work of Jesus Christ. This journey involves a transformation in this present life and the hope of eternal life in the age to come. It is a testament to God's power to restore and His deep love for humanity. His power doesn't just revive; it brings about a completely new, abundant, and eternal life.

4.5 Spiritual Israel: Christians Are Now God's People

The concept of Spiritual Israel denotes an important shift in God's covenantal relationship with humanity. It speaks to the radical inclusivity that Christ's redemptive work introduced, extending the scope of God's people beyond the physical descendants of Abraham to all those who share Abraham's faith in God.

The Old Covenant: Physical Israel

In the Old Testament, God's covenant people were primarily the physical descendants of Abraham. This covenant, marked by circumcision, solidified their status as God's chosen people (Genesis 17:10-14). They were to be a "kingdom of priests and a holy nation" (Exodus 19:6, ESV). God's relationship with Israel was always meant to be a demonstration to the world of His character and intentions.

However, Israel's history was marred by disobedience and rebellion against God. Despite God's patience and continual calls to repentance through His prophets, the nation repeatedly fell into idolatry and immorality. In Matthew 21:43, Jesus declared a profound truth to the Jewish religious leaders, "Therefore I tell you, the kingdom of God will be taken away from you and given to a people producing its fruits" (ESV).

The New Covenant: Spiritual Israel

The New Testament introduces the concept of Spiritual Israel. The life, death, and resurrection of Jesus Christ initiated a new covenant, where ethnicity and physical lineage were no longer the primary identifiers of God's people. This idea is expressed in Romans 2:28-29, "For no one is a Jew who is merely one outwardly, nor is circumcision outward and physical. But a Jew is one inwardly, and circumcision is a matter of the heart, by the Spirit, not by the letter" (ESV).

This new covenant is marked by faith in Jesus Christ, who fulfilled the Law (Matthew 5:17) and offered Himself as the perfect sacrifice for the sins of the world (John 1:29). Those who trust in Christ for salvation are adopted into God's family, irrespective of their ethnic or cultural background.

The Church: True Descendants of Abraham

Paul makes it clear in Galatians 3:7, "Know then that it is those of faith who are the sons of Abraham" (ESV). The true descendants of Abraham, then, are not those who can trace their physical lineage back to him, but those who share the faith of Abraham. This is a radical assertion, radically inclusive in its scope. Through faith in Christ, all believers, both Jews and Gentiles, are united into one body—the church—which is Spiritual Israel.

Implications of Being Spiritual Israel

As Spiritual Israel, the church now assumes the role that physical Israel held in the Old Testament, namely to be a "holy nation" and a "kingdom of priests" (1 Peter 2:9, ESV). This indicates that Christians are called to be holy, set apart for God's purposes, and to serve as mediators between God and the world, proclaiming His excellencies and sharing the good news of Christ.

Additionally, being a part of Spiritual Israel carries with it the promise of God's enduring presence, as revealed in Hebrews 13:5 (ESV): "I will never leave you nor forsake you." The promises of God once given to physical Israel now apply to all those who are in Christ.

In conclusion, the concept of Spiritual Israel underscores the unifying power of the gospel that breaks down racial, cultural, and social barriers. It emphasizes the necessity of faith in Christ and embodies the expansive, inclusive love of God.

4.6 Spiritual Regeneration (Palingenesia): A New Life in the Sinful Person

Spiritual regeneration, or palingenesia, is a Greek term used in the New Testament to denote the idea of a "new birth," "rebirth," or "renewal." It is a fundamental aspect of the Christian doctrine of redemption, encapsulating the transformation that takes place in an individual when they come to faith in Jesus Christ.

The Need for Regeneration

Humanity's sinfulness, as depicted in the Bible, necessitates regeneration. Romans 3:23 states, "for all have sinned and fall short of the glory of God" (ESV). This verse underscores the universal need for redemption, given that all of humanity has fallen short of God's perfect standard. Due to our sinful nature, we are spiritually dead and separated from God (Ephesians 2:1, ESV). Therefore, the process of regeneration is a necessity for our reconciliation with God and spiritual transformation.

The Process of Regeneration

In the Gospel of John, Jesus provides an in-depth explanation of spiritual regeneration. Speaking to Nicodemus, a Jewish religious leader, Jesus declares, "Truly, truly, I say to you, unless one is born again he cannot see the kingdom of God" (John 3:3, ESV). Here, Jesus employs the metaphor of birth to depict the radical transformation involved in spiritual regeneration.

Titus 3:5 states, "He saved us, not because of works done by us in righteousness, but according to His own mercy, by the washing of regeneration and renewal of the Holy Spirit" (ESV). This passage depicts regeneration as a divine act of mercy by God, rather than a result of human efforts. This transformative process is initiated and completed by the grace of God through the work of the Holy Spirit.

The Outcomes of Regeneration

When an individual experiences spiritual regeneration, they transition from spiritual death to spiritual life. In his letter to the Ephesians, the apostle Paul writes, "But God, being rich in mercy, because of the great love with which he loved us, even when we were dead in our trespasses, made us alive together with Christ" (Ephesians 2:4-5, ESV).

Regeneration is more than just an altering of behavior or an adoption of new religious rituals. It is the complete renewal of one's spiritual nature. Second Corinthians 5:17 affirms, "Therefore, if anyone is in Christ, he is a new creation. The old has passed away; behold, the new has come" (ESV).

Regeneration also involves a transformation of one's desires and priorities. As believers, we are given a new heart that seeks after God and a new mind that understands and appreciates God's truths (Ezekiel 36:26, Romans 12:2).

The Continual Nature of Regeneration

While the act of spiritual regeneration is a one-time event, the effects of this regeneration are ongoing. This process is known as sanctification, the continuous development in holiness and righteousness. As stated by Jesus, "the one who endures to the end will be saved" (Matthew 24:13, ESV).

Sanctification is a lifelong journey and a constant struggle against sin, but it is through this process that believers grow more into the likeness of Christ. It's important to note that perseverance doesn't earn salvation, but it's the proof and result of a genuine, regenerating faith.

In conclusion, the process of spiritual regeneration underscores God's power to redeem and transform the human heart. It is a testament to His unfathomable mercy and grace and stands as the foundational prerequisite for a genuine relationship with Him. The life of a believer is marked by this transformative process, which not only grants a new spiritual life but also sets one on a lifelong journey of becoming more like Christ.

Chapter 5: Our Part: Sharing in the Power of God

5.1 Understanding Our Position: Clay in the Potter's Hands

The metaphor of clay in the potter's hands is a profound biblical illustration that portrays the sovereign power of God and the humble position of humanity. As we endeavor to understand our position in God's grand narrative of redemption, this analogy offers invaluable insights.

The Potter and the Clay: A Biblical Image

In Jeremiah 18:1-6, God instructed the prophet Jeremiah to visit a potter's house. The message conveyed through this visit offers a deep understanding of God's sovereignty and our human responsibility. The passage reads, "So I went down to the potter's house, and there he was working at his wheel. And the vessel he was making of clay was spoiled in the potter's hand, and he reworked it into another vessel, as it seemed good to the potter to do" (Jeremiah 18:3-4, ASV).

This analogy demonstrates that just as a potter has power over the clay to shape it into any form he wishes, so too does God have power over His creation. He molds and shapes us according to His will and for His glory.

God's Sovereignty and Our Humility

Recognizing ourselves as clay in the potter's hands highlights our reliance on God. This perspective fosters humility, as it acknowledges that we are entirely dependent on Him for our being, purpose, and destiny. As expressed in Isaiah 64:8, "But now, O LORD, thou art our father; we are the clay, and thou our potter; and we all are the work of thy hand" (ASV).

This perception of ourselves as clay, formed and shaped by the ultimate Potter, reminds us of the immense gap between God's omnipotence and our human limitations. It fosters a sense of humility, reminding us of our need for God's direction and the surrender of our will to His.

The Shaping Process

While the metaphor underscores God's sovereignty, it also highlights the ongoing process of sanctification in a believer's life. God, the master potter, is continuously molding us into vessels of honor. This process, however, is not always easy. There are times when the potter must apply pressure, reshape, and even break the clay to make it into the vessel he desires.

Similarly, God uses circumstances, including trials and difficulties, to shape our character and make us more like Christ. As stated in Romans 5:3-4, "Not only that, but we rejoice in our sufferings, knowing that suffering produces endurance, and endurance produces character, and character produces hope" (ESV).

Our Response: Surrender and Trust

Understanding our position as clay in the Potter's hands calls for a response of surrender and trust. We are called to yield to God's will, trusting in His wisdom and goodness, even when His shaping process is uncomfortable or hard to understand.

As Proverbs 3:5-6 instructs, "Trust in the LORD with all your heart, and do not lean on your own understanding. In all your ways acknowledge him, and he will make straight your paths" (ESV). When we view ourselves as clay in the hands of the divine Potter, we learn to surrender our plans, desires, and understanding to Him, trusting Him to shape our lives according to His perfect design.

In conclusion, recognizing our position as clay in the Potter's hands is integral to sharing in the power of God. It teaches us humility, emphasizes the necessity of sanctification, and calls us to surrender and trust. Through this understanding, we are better equipped to cooperate with God's redemptive work in our lives and the world, echoing Paul's words in Philippians 2:12, "Therefore, my beloved, as you have always obeyed, so now, not only as in my presence but much more in my absence, work out your own salvation with fear and trembling" (ESV). This is our part in sharing God's power, as we allow Him to mold us according to His purpose and will.

5.2 Aligning with God's Will: The First Step to Power

Aligning ourselves with God's will is central to experiencing and sharing in God's power. This alignment is not a passive process, but an active, intentional commitment to seek and follow God's directives as revealed in the Holy Scriptures.

Understanding God's Will

The first step in aligning with God's will is gaining a clear understanding of what His will entails. This is where the inspired, inerrant Word of God serves as our primary guide. "All Scripture is breathed out by God and profitable for teaching, for reproof, for correction, and for training in righteousness" (2 Timothy 3:16, ESV). The Bible, as God's divinely inspired message, gives us comprehensive insight into His will for humanity and for our individual lives.

God's will is not only that we believe in Him and accept His Son Jesus Christ as our Lord and Savior (John 6:40, ESV), but also that we reflect His character and values in our daily living. He desires that we "walk in a manner worthy of the Lord, fully pleasing to him: bearing fruit in every good work and increasing in the knowledge of God" (Colossians 1:10, ESV).

The Challenge of Alignment

Aligning with God's will can be challenging. It requires us to set aside our desires and plans, submitting instead to God's directives. Our human nature often resists such submission, as it goes against the self-serving tendencies inherent in us. Nevertheless, the Bible admonishes us to "submit yourselves therefore to God" (James 4:7, ESV), and to "trust in the LORD with all your heart, and do not lean on your own understanding. In all your ways acknowledge him, and he will make straight your paths" (Proverbs 3:5-6, ESV).

Jesus Christ provides us with the perfect example of such submission and alignment with God's will. Despite the anguish and suffering He faced on the cross, He chose to submit to God's will, saying, "not my will, but yours, be done" (Luke 22:42, ESV). Jesus' obedience to God's will, even to the point of death, sets a powerful example for us to follow.

The Power in Alignment

Alignment with God's will is not only our duty as believers, but also the pathway to experiencing God's power. When we align our will with God's, we place ourselves in a position where God's power can work in and through us.

The apostle Paul, for example, experienced God's power when he aligned his life with God's will. Despite his past as a persecutor of Christians, Paul submitted to God's will and became a powerful instrument in spreading the Gospel. He acknowledged this when he wrote, "But by the grace of God I am what I am, and his grace toward me was not in vain. On the contrary, I worked harder than any of them, though it was not I, but the grace of God that is with me" (1 Corinthians 15:10, ESV).

This divine empowerment is available to every believer who aligns their will with God's. God's power, as Paul writes, "is made perfect in weakness" (2 Corinthians 12:9, ESV). When we acknowledge our human weakness and align ourselves with God's will, His power is manifested in us, enabling us to accomplish more than we could ever do in our strength.

In conclusion, aligning with God's will is crucial for experiencing and sharing in God's power. It involves understanding God's will, submitting to it despite the challenges, and positioning ourselves for divine empowerment. As we align our will with God's, we become partners in His divine mission, working with Him in advancing His kingdom on earth. While we do not believe the Holy Spirit miraculously indwells us, His inspired words guide us when we correctly understand and apply them in our lives, thereby allowing us to align with God's will and partake in His power.

God's perfect foreknowledge, reflecting what we will freely choose, ensures that our alignment with His will is an exercise of our free will, rather than predestined. This process of alignment and the resulting sharing in God's power underscore the reality that our salvation is a journey—a path we tread in obedience and faith, and not merely a condition or state of being. In the words of Jesus, "the one who endures to the end will be saved" (Matthew 24:13, ESV).

5.3 Active Faith: A Catalyst for Divine Power

Active faith plays a significant role in our sharing in the power of God. Faith, in the biblical sense, involves a profound conviction in God and His promises, coupled with a readiness to act on that belief. It is not merely passive agreement, but a dynamic, living commitment that moves us to action and results in transformative power.

Understanding Active Faith

The essence of active faith is beautifully encapsulated in James 2:14-26 (ESV). The passage emphasizes that faith without corresponding action is "dead." It vividly illustrates this point with the example of Abraham, whose faith led him to act in obedience to God, even when it meant offering his beloved son Isaac as a sacrifice. His faith was made "complete" by his actions (James 2:22).

This concept of faith is far from the notions of a passive belief or simple intellectual assent. It is an active, persistent faith that prompts action. Active faith means that we not only believe God's Word, but we also live by it. It propels us to act in line with our belief, shaping our attitudes, words, and deeds.

Active Faith and Divine Power

Active faith is a catalyst for divine power. This becomes evident when we consider some of the biblical narratives. For example, consider the woman suffering from a bleeding disorder in Mark 5:25-34 (ESV). Despite her condition and societal stigmatization, she reached out in faith to touch Jesus' garment, convinced that this action would result in her healing. Jesus confirmed her active faith by declaring, "Your faith has made you well."

The role of active faith in accessing divine power is further emphasized in Hebrews 11, often referred to as the "Hall of Faith." The chapter records the exploits of various biblical characters who, through their active faith, "conquered kingdoms, enforced justice, obtained promises, stopped the mouths of lions" (Hebrews 11:33, ESV). These extraordinary outcomes were not due to the individuals' personal strength or abilities, but due to the divine power accessed through their active faith.

Cultivating Active Faith

Cultivating active faith requires regular and diligent interaction with God's Word. Romans 10:17 (ESV) reminds us that "faith comes from hearing, and hearing through the word of Christ." As we spend time in Scripture, gaining a deep understanding of God's character and promises, our faith in Him grows. It's also essential to act on the truths we discover in His Word, for it is in the doing that our faith truly comes alive and becomes active.

As believers, we're called to a life of active faith, not passive belief. This faith isn't just an abstract concept; it has real-world implications. It requires us to step out of our comfort zones, take risks, and make sacrifices. But it also allows us to access and share in God's divine power. It doesn't make God a "slot machine" that dispenses blessings upon demand. Instead, it positions us to receive what God, in His perfect wisdom and timing, knows we need.

In conclusion, active faith is a fundamental aspect of sharing in God's power. It involves understanding and embracing God's Word, aligning our actions with His will, and persistently trusting in His promises. In a world that often values seeing over believing, active faith challenges us to believe first, thereby allowing us to see the manifestation of God's power. The divine power that results from our active faith confirms the truth that salvation is not a state, but a journey of enduring to the end. As Jesus affirmed, "the one who endures to the end will be saved" (Matthew 24:13, ESV).

5.4 The Power of Prayer: Communicating with the Divine

Prayer, an intimate conversation with our Creator, serves as one of the most significant ways in which we share in the power of God. It is a key component of our relationship with God, enabling us to express our deepest emotions, request divine intervention, and seek wisdom and guidance. However, it's essential to remember that prayer is not a means by which we manipulate God into doing our will, but rather a process through which we align ourselves with His divine will and purpose.

The Nature of Prayer

At its core, prayer is a dialogue with God. It is a two-way communication, involving both speaking to God and listening for His response through His Word and the circumstances of life. It is a time for expressing our feelings, confessing our sins, giving thanks, and presenting our requests to God. But prayer also involves a level of quietness and attentiveness, where we clear our minds of our concerns and focus on what God might be saying to us through His Word.

The model prayer given by Jesus in Matthew 6:9-13 (ESV), commonly known as the Lord's Prayer, provides a blueprint for effective communication with God. It begins with recognizing God's holiness ("Our Father in heaven, hallowed be your name"), expresses longing for His kingdom and will ("Your kingdom come, your will be done"), and asks for our daily needs ("Give us this day our daily bread"). It also includes confession and seeking forgiveness ("Forgive us our debts, as we also have forgiven our debtors"), as well as seeking protection from temptation ("And lead us not into temptation").

The Role of Prayer in Sharing God's Power

Prayer is the conduit through which we can share in God's power. This doesn't mean that God acts as a cosmic vending machine, dispensing whatever we request. Rather, prayer allows us to align our will with God's, resulting in actions that reflect His will and purpose.

The apostle Paul, in Philippians 4:6-7 (ESV), encourages us not to be anxious about anything but to present our requests to God in every situation through prayer and petition with thanksgiving. The peace of God, which surpasses all understanding, will guard our hearts and minds in Christ Jesus. This peace is a manifestation of the divine power we access through prayer.

Prayer also played a crucial role in the early church's experience of God's power. In Acts 4:31 (ESV), the disciples prayed for boldness to speak God's Word. In response, "the place in which they were gathered together was shaken, and they were all filled with the Holy Spirit and continued to speak the word of God with boldness." Here, we see the transformative power of prayer as it equipped the believers to share God's Word boldly.

Growing in Prayer

Cultivating a robust prayer life requires intentional practice. It involves setting aside regular time for prayer, being honest and open in our communication with God, and patiently waiting for His response. We should approach God with reverence, but also with the confidence of children coming to a loving Father (Hebrews 4:16, ESV).

Prayer is also an act of faith. We pray because we believe God hears us and will respond in accordance with His perfect will and timing. And while God in His omniscience already knows our needs and desires, He delights in our willingness to express them and to seek His guidance.

In conclusion, prayer is a powerful means through which we share in the divine power of God. It involves an intimate dialogue with our Creator, allowing us to express our innermost thoughts and feelings and to align our will with His. As we mature in our prayer life, we can experience an ever-deeper sense of God's peace, wisdom, and guidance, which are clear manifestations of His divine power. Prayer, then, is not only a spiritual discipline but also a divine gift that enables us to participate in God's work and share in His divine power.

5.5 The Bible: The Word of God Exerts Power

As Christians, we firmly believe that the Bible, the inspired Word of God, wields enormous power. In its pages, God reveals His character, His will, His purpose for humanity, and the path to salvation. Through studying the Bible, we can tap into divine wisdom and guidance, equipping us to navigate life's challenges and draw closer to our Creator.

The Bible as Inspired Word of God

We believe that "all Scripture is breathed out by God and profitable for teaching, for reproof, for correction, and for training in righteousness" (2 Timothy 3:16, ESV). This means that the human authors of the Bible were moved along by the Holy Spirit, ensuring that their writings are entirely accurate, reliable, and authoritative.

Each book in the Bible, while reflecting the unique style and context of its human author, carries the imprint of divine inspiration.

The Bible, in its entirety, tells a unified story of God's plan for humanity's redemption, culminating in the life, death, and resurrection of Jesus Christ.

The Transformative Power of God's Word

God's Word is not simply a repository of historical information or moral guidelines. It's a living, active force that can deeply impact our lives. Hebrews 4:12 (ESV) states, "For the word of God is living and active, sharper than any two-edged sword, piercing to the division of soul and of spirit, of joints and of marrow, and discerning the thoughts and intentions of the heart."

The Bible can convict us of sin, reveal God's standards of righteousness, guide our decision-making, and shape our worldview. As we study the Bible and apply its teachings, we find our attitudes, behaviors, and desires increasingly aligned with those of Christ.

The Bible as a Source of Divine Wisdom

The Bible is an indispensable resource for understanding God's perspective on life and human existence. It imparts divine wisdom that far surpasses human understanding. As we immerse ourselves in the Scriptures, we gain insight into God's character, His view of humanity, and His purpose for our lives.

Take, for instance, the wisdom literature in the Old Testament, which includes books like Proverbs and Ecclesiastes. These biblical texts provide guidance on diverse aspects of life, including relationships, work, justice, and the pursuit of happiness.

Interacting with the Word of God

Studying the Bible is not a passive activity. We must engage with the text, asking questions, seeking connections, reflecting on its implications, and applying its teachings in our lives. We must also approach the Bible prayerfully, asking God to illuminate our understanding.

The Bereans mentioned in Acts 17:11 (ESV) serve as an example in this regard. They received the apostle Paul's teachings with eagerness and "examined the Scriptures daily to see if these things were so." Their active engagement with the Scriptures enabled them to verify Paul's teaching and accept the gospel message.

The Bible and the Holy Spirit

While we reject the notion of the Holy Spirit miraculously indwelling in us to guide our understanding of the Bible, we do believe that the Spirit's influence is manifested in the Scriptures. It is through diligent and faithful study of the Word that the Spirit's guidance becomes apparent, helping us correctly understand and apply God's teachings.

The Bible, as the inspired Word of God, is not a static, lifeless text. It is a dynamic and powerful force that can transform our lives, providing us with divine wisdom and guidance. It is through our engagement with the Bible, rather than through miraculous or mystical experiences, that we can share in God's divine power. Understanding the power of the Word can thus encourage us to immerse ourselves more deeply in the study of the Scriptures and apply its teachings in our daily lives.

Thus, the Bible holds a central place in our Christian journey, equipping us to share in the power of God. It remains our guiding light, illuminating the path to the righteous life that God desires us to live.

5.6 Serving Others: Demonstrating God's Power in Us

God's power is at work in us when we serve others. As we engage in acts of service, we emulate Christ's model of humility, sacrifice, and love, thereby manifesting God's transformative power. This section explores how serving others demonstrates God's power in us and how it is integral to our Christian journey.

The Model of Christ

Jesus Christ is the perfect model of servitude. Despite being the Son of God, He humbled Himself to serve humanity. The Gospel of Mark records Jesus saying, "For even the Son of Man came not to be served but to serve, and to give his life as a ransom for many" (Mark 10:45, ESV). Christ's ultimate act of service was His willing sacrifice on the cross, demonstrating His immeasurable love for humanity.

The Call to Serve

As followers of Christ, we are called to serve others. Galatians 5:13 (ESV) says, "For you were called to freedom, brothers. Only do not use your freedom as an opportunity for the flesh, but through love serve one another." This means that our freedom in Christ is not for selfish gain, but it should be used to serve others in love, following Christ's example.

How Serving Others Manifests God's Power

1. **Transforms Our Character**: Serving others helps mold our character to be more like Christ's. As we engage in acts of service, we learn humility, selflessness, compassion, and love - traits that reflect God's character. This transformation is a demonstration of God's power at work in us.

2. **Impacts Lives**: When we serve others in Christ's name, we can make a profound impact on their lives. Acts of service can provide comfort, relief, hope, and love to those in need. This can lead others to recognize God's love and power, possibly drawing them closer to Him.

3. **Strengthens the Church Community**: Serving within the church strengthens the community of believers. As each person uses their God-given talents and abilities to serve, the body of Christ is edified, unified, and enabled to function effectively. "As each has received a gift, use it to serve one

another, as good stewards of God's varied grace" (1 Peter 4:10, ESV).

Service as a Response to God's Love

Our service to others should not be seen as a burdensome obligation but as a joyful response to God's love for us. Understanding God's sacrificial love, as displayed through Christ's death on the cross, motivates us to extend this love to others through acts of service.

Challenges in Serving Others

Serving others often requires self-sacrifice and can sometimes be difficult. We may face challenges such as indifference, rejection, or misunderstanding from those we seek to serve. Yet, it is through these difficulties that God's power is further displayed, enabling us to persevere and continue serving with love and humility.

Serving with Wisdom and Discernment

While we are called to serve others, it is crucial to do so with wisdom and discernment, guided by the principles of God's Word. We must ensure that our acts of service do not enable harmful behavior or contribute to dependence. Serving others effectively often involves helping them develop skills and abilities to improve their situation, rather than simply providing temporary relief.

Serving others is a profound demonstration of God's power at work in us. It molds our character, impacts lives, and strengthens the church community. As we serve, we follow Christ's example, reflect God's love, and become living testimonies of His transformative power. Indeed, service to others is a vital part of our Christian journey, a journey made possible by God's power at work in us.

Chapter 6: Harnessing the Power: The Word That Changes Lives

6.1 God's Word: A Powerful Weapon

As Christians, we are engaged in a spiritual battle. However, God, in His gracious providence, has provided us with a potent weapon—the Word of God. This section examines how God's Word functions as a powerful weapon in our lives, transforming us and equipping us for every spiritual conflict.

Understanding the Spiritual Battle

The Apostle Paul reminds us in Ephesians 6:12 (ESV), "For we do not wrestle against flesh and blood, but against the rulers, against the authorities, against the cosmic powers over this present darkness, against the spiritual forces of evil in the heavenly places." We are engaged in a spiritual battle, one that requires spiritual weapons. One of these is God's Word.

God's Word as a Weapon

The Word of God is not a conventional weapon; it is spiritual and more potent than any physical tool of combat. Hebrews 4:12 (ESV) attests to this, saying, "For the word of God is living and active, sharper than any two-edged sword, piercing to the division of soul and of spirit, of joints and of marrow, and discerning the thoughts and intentions of the heart." God's Word cuts through deceit, reveals truth, convicts hearts, and guides us to righteousness.

The Sword of the Spirit

In Ephesians 6:17 (ESV), Paul describes the Word of God as the "sword of the Spirit." As a sword, God's Word is an offensive weapon in our spiritual battles. It is instrumental in combating the lies, temptations, and deceptions thrown at us by the enemy. With it, we can resist the devil and stand firm in truth.

God's Word Transforms

God's Word is not only a weapon for defense but also a tool for transformation. Romans 12:2 (ESV) encourages us not to conform to the patterns of this world but be transformed by renewing our minds. The Word of God plays an integral role in this process. As we engage with Scripture, our minds are renewed, our perspectives changed, and our attitudes and behaviors gradually become more Christ-like. This transformative power underscores the dynamic nature of God's Word.

God's Word Equips

The Apostle Paul, in 2 Timothy 3:16-17 (ESV), writes, "All Scripture is breathed out by God and profitable for teaching, for reproof, for correction, and for training in righteousness, that the man of God may be complete, equipped for every good work." Through the Word of God, we are equipped for every good work, prepared to face every challenge, and trained to walk in righteousness. As we apply the Word in our lives, it serves as a guide, providing direction and insight for every decision we make.

Engaging with the Word

To wield this powerful weapon effectively, we need to engage with God's Word regularly. This involves consistent reading and studying of the Scriptures, meditation on its truths, and application of its principles in our lives. As Psalm 119:105 (ASV) states, "Thy word is a lamp unto my feet, and a light unto my path," indicating the importance of internalizing God's Word for guidance.

Praying the Word

Using God's Word in prayer is another way we utilize its power. When we pray according to God's Word, we align our desires with God's will, enabling us to pray confidently and effectively. Jesus, in John 15:7 (ESV), promises, "If you abide in me, and my words abide in you, ask whatever you wish, and it will be done for you." The Word's power, when fused with prayer, brings about God's will in our lives.

The Word of God is indeed a powerful weapon. It equips us for spiritual battles, transforms our lives, and guides us in the path of righteousness. As we engage with the Word, pray according to it, and apply its truths in our lives, we harness its power, resulting in a life-changing impact. This powerful weapon, entrusted to us, is a manifestation of God's immense love and an essential tool in our journey as followers of Christ. Thus, let us embrace the Word, immerse ourselves in its truth, and witness the transformative power it holds.

6.2 The Transformative Power of the Scriptures

The Scriptures bear an extraordinary power within their pages. Not only do they reveal God's character, guide our behavior, and proclaim salvation in Christ, but they also possess a transformative power that, when properly understood and applied, can reshape lives in profound ways.

The Living Word

One of the reasons why the Scriptures hold transformative power is due to their nature as the "living Word." The book of Hebrews affirms this by saying, "For the word of God is living and active, sharper than any two-edged sword, piercing to the division of soul and of spirit, of joints and of marrow, and discerning the thoughts and intentions of the heart" (Hebrews 4:12, ESV). The Word of God is alive; it speaks into our lives today just as powerfully as it did when it was first written.

Renewing of the Mind

A primary way the Scriptures transform us is through the renewing of our minds. As we engage deeply with God's Word, we begin to think differently. The Apostle Paul writes in Romans 12:2 (ESV), "Do not be conformed to this world, but be transformed by the renewal of your mind, that by testing you may discern what is the will of God, what is good and acceptable and perfect." The Word of God exposes us to divine truths, challenging our preconceptions and leading us to think and live more aligned with God's will.

Conviction and Correction

The Scriptures also transform us by bringing conviction and correction. They serve as a mirror, reflecting our lives in the light of God's standard. As we encounter the Word of God, it exposes our sin, convicts us, and points us toward repentance and transformation. In 2 Timothy 3:16 (ESV), Paul confirms this by saying, "All Scripture is breathed out by God and profitable for teaching, for reproof, for correction, and for training in righteousness."

Inspiration to Action

The transformative power of the Scriptures isn't just about personal change; it also inspires action. The Bible is full of examples of individuals who, after encountering God's Word, were moved to act boldly and decisively. As we immerse ourselves in the Scriptures, we are empowered to live out our faith in practical and impactful ways.

Guidance for Life

The Scriptures offer guidance for life's journey, illuminating the path before us. They provide wisdom for decision-making, comfort in times of distress, and hope for the future. As David declares in Psalm 119:105 (ASV), "Thy word is a lamp unto my feet, And light unto my path." The Word of God gives direction to our lives, shaping our decisions and actions in line with God's purposes.

Growth in Godliness

As we meditate on the Scriptures, internalize their truths, and put them into practice, we experience growth in godliness. This spiritual growth is a transformative process that brings us closer to Christ's likeness. As we read in 2 Peter 3:18 (ESV), "But grow in the grace and knowledge of our Lord and Savior Jesus Christ." The transformative power of the Scriptures enables us to grow in our understanding of God and in our character.

The transformative power of the Scriptures is truly remarkable. The Word of God is a living, active force that reshapes our thinking, convicts and corrects us, inspires us to act, guides our lives, and fosters spiritual growth. As we commit ourselves to regular engagement with the Scriptures, we can expect a transformative work in our lives that reflects the power of God.

6.3 Meditating on the Word: Key to Spiritual Growth

Engaging with the Bible is more than just a passive reading experience—it's an active immersion in the Word of God that can stimulate spiritual growth and transformation. Meditating on the Word is a key practice in this process, enabling us to absorb and apply the biblical truths deeply and meaningfully.

The Practice of Biblical Meditation

Biblical meditation involves deep, reflective thought on the Scriptures, with the intention of understanding and applying God's Word in our lives. Unlike some forms of meditation that encourage emptying the mind, biblical meditation is about filling our minds with God's Word.

The Bible encourages meditation as a spiritual discipline. Joshua 1:8 (ASV) says, "This book of the law shall not depart out of thy mouth, but thou shalt meditate therein day and night, that thou mayest observe to do according to all that is written therein: for then thou shalt make thy way prosperous, and then thou shalt have good success." The benefits of meditation are clear: prosperity and success in God's terms, achieved through careful contemplation and application of His Word.

Benefits of Meditating on the Word

Meditating on the Word brings several benefits. First, it promotes a deeper understanding of Scripture. When we meditate, we take time to ponder on the Word, often gaining new insights and revelations that a cursory reading may not provide.

Second, meditation facilitates personal application. As we reflect on Scripture, we think about how it relates to our own circumstances, enabling us to apply the Word in our everyday lives.

Third, meditation nurtures spiritual growth. As we fill our minds with God's Word and allow it to penetrate our hearts, we become more attuned to God's will, prompting us to live more Christ-like lives.

Finally, meditating on the Word brings us closer to God. It's a spiritual practice that deepens our relationship with Him, as we focus our minds on His Word and open our hearts to His presence.

How to Meditate on the Word

The practice of meditating on the Word involves several steps. First, select a passage of Scripture. Consider passages that have particularly touched you or those that address areas in your life where you seek guidance.

Next, read the passage slowly and attentively. Absorb each word and phrase, allowing the message to resonate with you. Read it several times to familiarize yourself with its content and context.

Then, reflect on the passage. What does it reveal about God? What does it say about human nature or the nature of the world? How does it apply to your life? What does it mean for your beliefs and actions?

After reflecting, respond to the Word. This might involve prayer, confession, worship, or commitment to action. The response should be personal and heartfelt, flowing from the understanding gained through meditation.

Finally, rest in the Word. Take some time to be silent before God, allowing the Scripture to settle in your heart. This is a time of intimate communion with God, where His Word begins to transform you from within.

Challenges and Persistence

Meditating on the Word can be challenging. Our minds can easily wander, and the demands of daily life can make it difficult to find the time. However, like any discipline, persistence is key. The more we practice, the more natural it becomes, and the more we benefit from it.

David, the Psalmist, expressed the essence of this discipline when he wrote, "Oh, how I love your law! It is my meditation all the day" (Psalm 119:97, ASV). Let us strive to have the same love for God's Word, meditating on it day and night, and experiencing the spiritual growth that it brings. Remember, it's not the reading of many books that brings wisdom, but the regular, reflective reading of one—the Bible—that makes the difference.

As we engage with Scripture through meditation, we're not simply gaining knowledge, but cultivating a deeper relationship with God. We're allowing the inspired, inerrant Word of God to shape us, to guide us, to transform us. Let the Word of God take root in your life through the practice of biblical meditation, and watch as it nurtures an incredible spiritual growth, bringing you closer to the image of Christ.

6.4 In-Depth Study of God's Word: Getting at What the Bible Authors Meant by the Word that They Used

Interpreting and understanding Scripture is more than just reading. It's a deep dive into language, context, culture, and the specific meaning of words to uncover what the biblical authors truly intended to convey. This in-depth study, also known as exegesis, can significantly enhance our grasp of the Word of God and our spiritual growth.

Understanding Word Meaning in Context

The key to comprehending the authors' intent is by considering the word meaning within its specific context. Every word in the Bible was written in a particular linguistic, cultural, historical, and literary context. Hence, it's crucial to understand these contexts to gain a precise meaning of the words used.

For example, the word "love" in English has a broad range of meanings, but Greek, the language of the New Testament, has four different words for "love," each with its unique nuance. Understanding the specific Greek word used can provide a more accurate understanding of the text. For instance, when Jesus said, "love your enemies" (Matthew 5:44, ESV), He used the Greek word "agapao," referring to a selfless, sacrificial love that seeks the best for others, regardless of their actions towards us. Such understanding brings a deeper richness to Jesus' commandment.

Exegetical Tools and Techniques

To study the Bible in-depth, a variety of tools and techniques can be employed. Lexicons can provide detailed definitions of Hebrew and Greek words. Concordances can show where a word is used throughout Scripture, enabling us to compare usage and grasp a fuller meaning. Commentaries written by respected scholars can provide insight into the cultural and historical context of a passage.

However, it is vital to approach these tools with discernment. We should carefully select resources that uphold the Bible as the inspired, inerrant Word of God, avoiding those that lean towards higher criticism or a liberal-moderate perspective.

Illustrating the Process

To illustrate the process of in-depth study, let's consider the word "repent." This English word can suggest feelings of sorrow or regret, but in the New Testament, the Greek word "metanoia" is often translated as "repent." It means a change of mind or a transformative change of heart.

In Matthew 3:2, John the Baptist proclaimed, "Repent, for the kingdom of heaven is at hand" (ESV). To understand John's call, we must grasp the depth of "metanoia." It's not merely about feeling sorry for sins but signifies a total transformation of one's mind and life direction—turning away from sin and turning toward God.

The Role of the Holy Spirit

While we can use tools and techniques for in-depth study, we should remember that the Holy Spirit played a crucial role in inspiring the authors of the Bible. Although the Holy Spirit does not miraculously indwell us to guide us in understanding the Bible and making decisions, it is the Holy Spirit inspired words that guide us when we have a correct understanding of them and apply them in a balanced manner.

A Life-Changing Journey

The process of in-depth Bible study can be a challenging yet rewarding journey. It requires time, effort, patience, and prayer. However, the fruits of this discipline are worth the investment. As we begin to understand the original intent of the biblical authors, our understanding of God's Word deepens, our relationship with God strengthens, and our lives transform.

Indeed, the Word of God is living and active, sharper than any two-edged sword, and it discerns the thoughts and intentions of the heart (Hebrews 4:12, ESV). So, as we delve deeper into its riches, let's remember that the ultimate goal is not merely knowledge but a changed life—a life that reflects the love and wisdom of our Creator.

In summary, in-depth Bible study is a crucial discipline for every believer. It provides a foundation for understanding the original meaning of Scripture and equips us for a life of faith and godliness. So, let's take up this enriching endeavor, for in doing so, we are not merely studying a book, but we are seeking to know the heart of God Himself.

6.5 Living Out the Word: A Daily Challenge

The Bible, the inspired Word of God, is not just a compilation of historical events, poetry, prophecies, and letters. It is a guide for our daily lives—a timeless source of wisdom, comfort, correction, and encouragement. But to harness the transformative power of God's Word, it must move from our heads to our hearts, and from our hearts to our actions. Living out the Word is the challenge that every Christian faces daily.

The Word as a Mirror

James 1:22-25 (ESV) admonishes, "But be doers of the word, and not hearers only, deceiving yourselves. For if anyone is a hearer of the word and not a doer, he is like a man who looks intently at his natural face in a mirror... But the one who looks into the perfect law, the law of liberty, and perseveres, being no hearer who forgets but a doer who acts, he will be blessed in his doing." God's Word acts as a mirror that reveals who we truly are, exposing areas where we fall short. As we allow the Word to correct and guide us, we begin to see changes in our lives, aligning more closely with God's character.

Practical Steps for Living out the Word

Living out the Word involves application. This means taking the principles and precepts we learn from Scripture and implementing them in our daily life. Here are some practical steps that can help us achieve this:

- **Consistent Bible Study**: Regularly studying the Bible equips us with knowledge of God's will, helps us gain wisdom, and strengthens our faith. As we study, it's important to reflect and ask, "What is God's message for me in this passage?" and then apply it to our lives.
- **Prayer**: While the Holy Spirit does not miraculously guide us, we can seek God's wisdom in understanding His Word and the courage to apply it in our lives through prayer. It is through prayer that we maintain a personal relationship with God, seeking His will in our life.
- **Fellowship with Other Believers**: Sharing insights and experiences with fellow Christians can provide added encouragement and accountability. Through fellowship, we can "spur one another on toward love and good deeds" (Hebrews 10:24, ESV).
- **Serving Others**: The Bible teaches us to serve others selflessly, following the example of Jesus. By putting others' needs before our own, we are living out God's Word in a practical way.

Challenges and Encouragement

Living out the Word can be challenging. It often requires us to go against our human nature and the trends of the society around us. But we are not left to face these challenges alone. God is with us, providing strength and guidance as we seek to follow His Word.

We can draw encouragement from Joshua 1:8 (ASV), "This book of the law shall not depart out of thy mouth, but thou shalt meditate thereon day and night, that thou mayest observe to do according to all that is written therein: for then thou shalt make thy way prosperous, and then thou shalt have good success." When we consistently meditate on and apply God's Word, He promises to guide and bless us.

The Transformative Power of the Word

Living out God's Word daily is not about performing religious duties—it's about experiencing transformation. As we apply the truths in Scripture, our thoughts, attitudes, and actions begin to reflect God's character. We become the "light of the world," impacting others around us with the love and truth of God (Matthew 5:14, ESV).

In conclusion, God's Word is not meant to be just read and heard but lived. Living out the Word is indeed a daily challenge, but it's also an exciting journey of growth and transformation. As we make the choice every day to allow God's Word to shape our lives, we witness its true power—the power to change lives, starting with our own.

6.6 The Word of God and You: The Bible Is Authentic and True

The Bible stands as a unique testament among religious texts, serving as the inspired, inerrant, and infallible Word of God. It has weathered the storms of historical scrutiny, philosophical arguments, and countless criticisms, yet it remains an unshaken beacon of truth. It offers a clear, coherent message of God's love, grace, and justice, presented through diverse human authors moved along by the Holy Spirit over the span of approximately 1,600 years. In this section, we will explore the Bible's authenticity and how it profoundly impacts you.

The Authenticity of the Bible: Historical, Prophetic, and Archaeological Evidences

From a historical perspective, the Bible has proven to be reliable. It records events, individuals, and places that have been substantiated by extrabiblical historical documents and archaeological findings. Despite being penned over several centuries, it exhibits a remarkable consistency in its message and teachings, something one would expect from a divine source of truth.

Prophetically, the Bible distinguishes itself by making detailed predictions that have come true. Prophecies about the Messiah, the fate of nations, and end-times events have been fulfilled with stunning accuracy, proving its divine origin. Yet, the Bible doesn't teach the restoration of physical Israel in the last days. Jesus pronounced that the "kingdom of God will be taken away from you [the Jews] and given to a people [Spiritual Israel, Christians] producing its fruits" (Matt 21:43, ESV). God's true people today are those who follow Christ, regardless of their ethnic or national identity.

Archaeologically, findings continue to validate biblical accounts, confirming the historicity of biblical events and figures. For example, the discovery of the Hittite civilization, the existence of King David, and the city of Jericho align with biblical narratives.

Understanding the Bible Correctly: A Conservative, Balanced Approach

The objective Historical-Grammatical Method of interpretation seeks to understand the text as the original audience would have understood it, taking into account the historical and cultural context. This approach respects the Bible as a divine-human book. While acknowledging the human authors' styles and backgrounds, it upholds the Bible's divine inspiration, thereby treating it as an integrated, coherent text.

The Impact of the Bible's Authenticity on You

The authenticity and truth of the Bible have profound implications for our lives. First, it assures us that God has spoken, revealing His nature, purposes, and will for humanity. Thus, we can confidently turn to the Bible for guidance, wisdom, and comfort.

Second, the Bible provides a foundation for our faith. As Paul wrote in Romans 10:17 (ESV), "So faith comes from hearing, and hearing through the word of Christ." The more we delve into God's Word, the stronger our faith becomes.

Lastly, the truth of the Bible holds us accountable. Hebrews 4:12 (ESV) declares, "For the word of God is living and active, sharper than any two-edged sword, piercing to the division of soul and of spirit, of joints and of marrow, and discerning the thoughts and intentions of the heart." It challenges us to align our lives with God's standards and transforms us as we yield to its teachings.

In conclusion, the Bible's authenticity and truth are not merely academic or theological points—they are life-changing realities. When we approach the Bible with reverence, respect, and a readiness to yield to its truths, we unlock the transformative power of God's Word in our lives. God's Word is not just information; it's transformation. It's not merely to be dissected and discussed but believed and obeyed. It's not just a relic of the past, but a living, active, and relevant guide for our lives today. Embrace the Word of God and let it shape you, guide you, and mold you as you journey through life, knowing with assurance that "the one who endures to the end will be saved" (Matt 24:13, ESV).

Chapter 7: The Divine Blueprint: God's Power in His Laws

7.1 Understanding God's Laws: A Reflection of His Power

In the universe's grand architecture, we find a testament to the power and wisdom of God. Each law that governs the natural world, each principle that undergirds human relationships, each moral standard that instructs us in righteousness—each is a reflection of His power, and each provides insight into His character. This divine blueprint is most comprehensively expressed in the Bible, where God's laws are revealed in all their breadth and depth.

God's Laws: A Mirror of His Nature

In God's laws, we encounter a mirror of His own nature. The Ten Commandments, for instance, illustrate His perfect holiness, justice, and love. The laws regarding love for God (Exodus 20:3-11, ASV) reflect His uniqueness and supremacy. Laws about love for neighbor (Exodus 20:12-17, ASV) demonstrate His concern for justice, integrity, and the sanctity of human relationships.

It's crucial to understand that God's laws are not arbitrary, nor are they oppressive. They reflect His character and wisdom and are designed for our good. For instance, when we read in Proverbs 14:34 (ESV), "Righteousness exalts a nation, but sin is a reproach to any people," we see the beneficial effect of righteousness on a society.

God's Laws: Tools of Divine Power

God's laws are not passive—they actively shape creation and guide our lives. They express His sovereignty and maintain order in the universe. Just as natural laws like gravity and thermodynamics shape the physical world, God's moral and spiritual laws shape the moral universe.

Consider God's law of sowing and reaping expressed in Galatians 6:7-8 (ESV), "Do not be deceived: God is not mocked, for whatever one sows, that will he also reap. For the one who sows to his own flesh will from the flesh reap corruption, but the one who sows to the Spirit will from the Spirit reap eternal life." This law is a divine principle of cause and effect, revealing how God's moral order works.

God's Laws: A Guide for Life

God's laws serve as a guide for life, providing us with wisdom and instruction for navigating life's complexities. They teach us about God's standards, our obligations, and the consequences of our actions. In Psalm 119:105 (ASV), the psalmist beautifully describes God's law as "a lamp unto my feet, and a light unto my path," symbolizing how His laws illuminate our way and guide us through life's darkest valleys.

When we live in accordance with God's laws, we experience blessings and fulfillment. Deuteronomy 30:16 (ASV) promises, "in that I command thee this day to love Jehovah thy God, to walk in his ways, and to keep his commandments and his statutes and his ordinances, that thou mayest live and multiply, and that Jehovah thy God may bless thee in the land whither thou goest in to possess it." God's laws are not burdensome but are designed for our good, leading us to life in its fullness.

God's Laws: Pointers to Salvation

God's laws also serve a crucial role in showing us our need for salvation. Romans 3:20 (ESV) explains, "For by works of the law no human being will be justified in his sight, since through the law comes knowledge of sin." The law exposes our sinfulness, driving us to Christ, who alone fulfilled the law and offers grace and mercy to those who trust in Him.

Remember, the laws of God are not about earning salvation through works but understanding our need for grace and responding in faith and obedience. Ephesians 2:8-10 (ESV) clearly states that we are saved by grace through faith, and not by works, so that no one can boast. However, we are also created for good works, which God has prepared for us to walk in—these works being the fruit of our faith and obedience to His law.

God's Laws: Lasting and Inerrant

God's laws are not outdated relics from an ancient world; they're timeless and universal, as applicable today as they were when first delivered to humanity. Jesus affirmed this in Matthew 5:17-18 (ESV), "Do not think that I have come to abolish the Law or the Prophets; I have not come to abolish them but to fulfill them. For truly, I say to you, until heaven and earth pass away, not an iota, not a dot, will pass from the Law until all is accomplished."

While some of the ceremonial and civil laws given to ancient Israel were specific to that time and context, the moral law—the reflection of God's character—remains applicable to all people, in all cultures, at all times.

Understanding God's laws is about more than adhering to rules—it's about understanding His character, His order, His wisdom, and His power. It's about recognizing our need for a Savior, living in harmony with His design, and experiencing the fullness of life He offers. So, we read, study, and meditate on His laws, treasuring them in our hearts that we might not sin against Him (Psalm 119:11, ASV) and enduring in faith until the end, for, as Jesus promised, "the one who endures to the end will be saved" (Matt 24:13, ESV).

7.2 The Ten Commandments: The Pillars of God's Authority

The Ten Commandments as Universal Principles

While the Mosaic Law, including the Ten Commandments, was specific to the Israelites, the principles they embody remain relevant to Christians. These commandments reflect the moral attributes of God, His character, and His standards of righteousness, providing a roadmap for ethical conduct and moral behavior.

The Enduring Principles of the Ten Commandments

Even though Christians are not under the Mosaic Law, the principles represented in the Ten Commandments still serve as a guide to living a life pleasing to God. As Paul writes in Romans 13:8-10 (ESV), "The one who loves another has fulfilled the law... Love does no wrong to a neighbor; therefore love is the fulfilling of the law." Let's examine these principles in the context of the New Testament.

1. **Exclusive Devotion to God**: Although Christians are not bound by the prohibition against making "graven images," the principle of putting God first and avoiding idolatry remains valid. Anything that takes priority over God in our lives can become an idol.

2. **Respect for God's Name**: Christians are encouraged to honor God in all they do, which includes respecting His name. Misusing God's name shows a lack of reverence for Him. Not using God's name, Jehovah, that he gave us 6,828 times as יהוה (JHVH), usually referred to as the Tetragrammaton (i.e., "having four letters") is also disrespectful.

3. **Observing the Sabbath**: While Christians are not obligated to observe the Sabbath on a specific day, the principle of setting aside regular time for rest and worship remains important.

4. **Honor Parents**: The principle of honoring one's parents is reiterated in the New Testament (Ephesians 6:1-3, ESV). This honor extends to respecting all those in positions of authority.

5. **Respect for Life**: The prohibition against murder underlines the sanctity of life, a principle that extends to harboring hatred in one's heart (Matthew 5:21-22, ESV).

6. **Fidelity in Marriage**: The commandment against adultery underscores the sanctity of marriage. Jesus expanded this in Matthew 5:27-28 (ESV) to include even lustful thoughts.

7. **Respect for Property**: The prohibition against stealing emphasizes the respect for others' property. This extends to being honest in all our dealings and respecting the rights of others.

8. **Truthfulness**: The commandment against bearing false witness underscores the importance of truthfulness. This principle is a key part of Christian ethics, as lies and deceit harm relationships and society.

9. **Contentment**: The commandment against coveting teaches contentment and warns against greed and envy, principles that are echoed in the teachings of Jesus and the apostles.

While we are no longer under the Mosaic Law, the moral principles these commandments encapsulate continue to guide Christian conduct. They provide a moral framework that reflects God's nature and character and following them is an expression of our love for God and for our neighbor. As Jesus stated in Matthew 22:37-40 (ESV), "You shall love the Lord your God with all your heart and with all your soul and with all your mind. This is the great and first commandment. And a second is like it: You shall love your neighbor as yourself. On these two commandments depend all the Law and the Prophets."

7.3 Laws of Love: God's Power in Relationships

In the heart of God's divine blueprint for humanity, the law of love occupies a central position. As the Apostle Paul attests in Romans 13:10 (ESV), "Love does no wrong to a neighbor; therefore love is the fulfilling of the law." This principle underlines the true power of God in relationships and offers an extraordinary perspective on how God's laws were designed to operate in a relational context.

The Supremacy of Love in God's Law

The teachings of Jesus Christ offer a profound revelation of how love operates as the core principle of God's law. Christ encapsulates the entire law into two commandments that hinge on love. In Matthew 22:37-40 (ESV), Jesus states, "You shall love the Lord your God with all your heart and with all your soul and with all your mind. This is the great and first commandment. And a second is like it: You shall love your neighbor as yourself. On these two commandments depend all the Law and the Prophets."

This directive outlines love as a guiding force behind God's laws, signaling its fundamental role in the divine blueprint. Our relationship with God is rooted in love, and this love cascades into our relationships with others, manifesting as acts of kindness, compassion, and respect.

Love in Relationships: A Reflection of Divine Principles

The dynamics of human relationships are varied and complex, but God's law provides a solid framework to navigate these complexities. The Apostle Paul paints a vivid portrait of love in 1 Corinthians 13:4-7 (ESV): "Love is patient and kind; love does not envy or boast; it is not arrogant or rude. It does not insist on its own way; it is not irritable or resentful; it does not rejoice at wrongdoing but rejoices with the truth. Love bears all things, believes all things, hopes all things, endures all things."

Here, Paul presents the law of love as a mirror of God's character, and as Christians, we are called to reflect this character in our relationships. The attributes of love detailed in this passage aren't just idealistic sentiments; they are practical guides to daily interactions, as applicable today as they were in the 1st century C.E.

The Transformative Power of Love

Jesus' teachings urge us to extend love even to those who may be difficult to love, including our enemies. In Matthew 5:43-48 (ESV), Jesus challenges conventional wisdom, saying, "You have heard that it was said, 'You shall love your neighbor and hate your enemy.' But I say to you, Love your enemies and pray for those who persecute you." This commandment, while counterintuitive to human nature, demonstrates the transformative power of God's love.

God's love transcends human boundaries and expectations, and when we apply this love in our relationships, we echo the divine blueprint in our lives. This doesn't imply a passive acceptance of mistreatment but represents a proactive stance of goodwill that can disarm hostility and promote reconciliation.

The Interconnection of Love and Freedom

In Galatians 5:13-14 (ESV), Paul declares, "For you were called to freedom, brothers. Only do not use your freedom as an opportunity for the flesh, but through love serve one another. For the whole law is fulfilled in one word: 'You shall love your neighbor as yourself.'" Here, Paul connects love and freedom, indicating that God's law, far from being a restrictive set of rules, is a path to true freedom.

When we live by the law of love, we find a freedom that isn't characterized by self-indulgence but by self-giving. This is the freedom Christ exemplified in his life and teachings, a freedom that reflects God's character and embodies His laws.

Love: The Binding Force

In sum, love, as it is described in the Bible, is not merely an emotion; it is an action, a commitment, and a way of life that reflects God's divine blueprint for human relationships. It is the binding force of God's commandments, guiding our interactions with God and others. It is the fulfillment of the law, reflecting God's power in relationships and demonstrating the essence of His divine blueprint for humanity.

As we grow in our understanding of this law of love, we find that it has the power to transform our relationships, bringing them into alignment with God's purpose. We begin to reflect the character of God in our interactions with others, embodying the principles of kindness, patience, humility, and selflessness that underpin God's laws. It is in this journey of love that we truly experience God's power in relationships, reflecting His divine blueprint in our lives.

7.4 God's Laws: Let God's Laws and Principles Train Your Conscience

One significant aspect of the divine blueprint of God's power in His laws is the transformation of our conscience through these laws and principles. An in-depth exploration of how God's laws can train our conscience is thus critical in understanding this blueprint. The conscience is a faculty of the human mind that discerns right from wrong and prompts us to act accordingly.

The Role of God's Laws in Shaping Conscience

The Scriptures, being the inspired and inerrant Word of God, serve as the ultimate standard of truth that trains our conscience. The Apostle Paul, in 2 Timothy 3:16-17 (ESV), affirms, "All Scripture is breathed out by God and profitable for teaching, for reproof, for correction, and for training in righteousness, that the man of God may be complete, equipped for every good work."

This is an explicit endorsement of the role of God's laws and principles in instructing and correcting us, thereby molding our conscience. However, this doesn't imply an automatic understanding or awareness of these laws. Our conscience needs continuous training through persistent engagement with the Scriptures.

Training the Conscience: Reading, Understanding, Applying

How can we train our conscience through God's laws? It begins with diligent reading of God's Word. However, merely reading isn't sufficient. We must also strive for understanding. As Proverbs 4:7 (ASV) advises, "Wisdom is the principal thing; therefore get wisdom; yea, with all thy getting get understanding."

Understanding isn't merely an intellectual grasp of God's laws; it is about discerning their relevance to our lives and seeing how they reflect God's character and His will for humanity. Such understanding comes when we seek God's wisdom and allow the Holy Spirit-inspired words to guide us.

After understanding, we must then apply God's laws in our daily lives. James 1:22-25 (ESV) exhorts us, "But be doers of the word, and not hearers only, deceiving yourselves... the one who looks into the perfect law, the law of liberty, and perseveres, being no hearer who forgets but a doer who acts, he will be blessed in his doing." Application is the final and crucial step in training our conscience.

Conscience and Freedom

Far from being an oppressive force, the training of our conscience through God's laws sets us free. As Jesus Christ declares in John 8:31-32 (ESV), "If you abide in my word, you are truly my disciples, and you will know the truth, and the truth will set you free." This freedom isn't a license to live according to our whims, but the power to live in alignment with God's divine blueprint.

God's laws train our conscience to discern and live out the truth, liberating us from the bondage of sin and self-deception.

Consequently, this freedom brings us into harmony with God and allows us to live fulfilling and impactful lives, a manifestation of the divine blueprint in our personal and communal experience.

Training the Conscience: A Lifelong Journey

Training the conscience is a lifelong journey. As believers, we must continually let God's laws and principles guide us. It isn't a once-for-all event, but a process that continues as long as we journey in faith. It requires humility, as we acknowledge our limitations and errors; diligence, as we persistently engage with God's Word; and courage, as we live out these laws in a world that often doesn't understand or appreciate them.

Through this process, we become, as Paul envisages in Ephesians 4:15 (ESV), "speaking the truth in love... grow up in every way into him who is the head, into Christ." The training of our conscience through God's laws isn't a mere moral improvement; it is part of our growth into the likeness of Christ, an embodiment of God's divine blueprint.

In conclusion, God's laws and principles play a crucial role in training our conscience. These laws, as revealed in the Scriptures, shape our moral discernment and guide our actions. As we engage with these laws – reading, understanding, and applying them – our conscience is trained to align with God's divine blueprint. This process is lifelong, requiring humility, diligence, and courage. Ultimately, through the training of our conscience, we are not only transformed individually but are also empowered to reflect God's character and purpose in our relationships, thus realizing God's divine blueprint in our lives.

7.5 Prophetic Laws: God's Sovereign Power Over Time

In studying the divine blueprint of God's power in His laws, we arrive at a crucial aspect: God's prophetic laws. This topic encompasses the understanding of God's sovereignty over time and history, His foreknowledge, and the role of prophecy in revealing His plan and purpose for humanity.

God's Sovereign Power Over Time and History

The Scripture presents God as sovereign over time and history. This sovereignty is founded on His timeless and omniscient nature. As the Psalmist declares, "From everlasting to everlasting, thou art God" (Psalm 90:2 ASV). God stands outside of time, and therefore He has total control over it.

This sovereign power over time is also evidenced in His governance of human history. Isaiah 46:10 (ASV) affirms: "Declaring the end from the beginning, and from ancient times the things that are not yet done; saying, My counsel shall stand, and I will do all my pleasure." This asserts God's capacity to direct history toward His intended ends.

God's Foreknowledge and Human Freedom

God's sovereignty over time and His foreknowledge of future events do not, however, negate human freedom. His foreknowledge merely reflects what individuals will freely choose. It doesn't dictate or determine human actions. As Peter explained on the day of Pentecost: "This Jesus, delivered up according to the definite plan and foreknowledge of God, you crucified and killed by the hands of lawless men" (Acts 2:23 ESV). The "lawless men" acted out of their own volition, yet their actions fell within God's foreknowledge.

The Role of Prophecy

God's prophetic laws reveal His sovereign control over time and His foreknowledge. Through the prophets, God unveiled His plans and purposes to humanity, manifesting His sovereignty over history.

The book of Daniel provides a comprehensive view of this. Nebuchadnezzar's dream in Daniel 2 and Daniel's vision in Daniel 7 (ASV) outline the successive world empires leading to God's everlasting kingdom. These prophecies show God's sovereign orchestration of human history.

Moreover, the prophecies of the Messiah in the Old Testament, fulfilled in Jesus Christ, show God's prophetic laws at work. As Isaiah prophesied: "For unto us a child is born, unto us a son is given; and the government shall be upon his shoulder: and his name shall be called Wonderful, Counselor, Mighty God, Everlasting Father, Prince of Peace" (Isaiah 9:6 ASV). This prophecy was fulfilled in the birth, life, death, and resurrection of Jesus Christ.

The fulfillment of prophecy verifies God's sovereign control over time and history, reinforcing the reliability and inerrancy of Scripture as God's inspired Word. It assures us that God's divine blueprint is unfolding as He purposed.

Application for the Believer

The knowledge of God's prophetic laws has profound implications for believers. It assures us of God's control in the midst of world events, even when they seem chaotic or uncertain. This knowledge encourages us to trust in God's providential care, knowing that He works "all things together for good, for those who are called according to his purpose" (Romans 8:28 ESV).

Moreover, it underscores the importance of aligning ourselves with God's divine blueprint. As we navigate through life, we must bear in mind God's prophetic laws, living in the present in light of His revealed future. This demands a diligent study of God's Word, seeking to understand and apply His laws and principles.

Conclusion

In conclusion, God's prophetic laws reveal His sovereign power over time and history. Through His foreknowledge and the fulfillment of prophecies, God demonstrates His control over the course of human history. As believers, the understanding of these prophetic laws enables us to trust in God's providence and align ourselves with His divine blueprint. It encourages us to live in the present with a keen awareness of God's plan and purpose for humanity. Thus, God's prophetic laws are integral to the divine blueprint, unveiling His power in His laws.

7.6 God's Moral Laws: The Power of Righteous Living

Within God's divine blueprint, His moral laws are foundational. These laws are more than mere ethical guidelines. They are revelations of God's own character, directing us toward righteous living that reflects His image.

The Nature of God's Moral Laws

God's moral laws are universal and timeless principles governing human behavior and attitudes. Rooted in God's unchanging character, they are not limited by culture, context, or chronology. The Ten Commandments, revealed to Moses, epitomize these moral laws (Exodus 20:1-17, ASV). They outline the basic requirements for a godly, righteous life, including honoring God, respecting life, and promoting justice, honesty, and purity. Yet, it's crucial to understand that while the Mosaic Law was specific to the Israelites, its underlying principles remain relevant to Christians.

The Purpose of God's Moral Laws

God's moral laws serve several interconnected purposes:

1. **Revealing God's Character:** God's moral laws provide a glimpse into His holy and righteous character. As 1 Peter 1:16 (ESV) states, "You shall be holy, for I am holy."

2. **Guiding Righteous Living:** These laws show us how to live a life pleasing to God. As the Psalmist declares, "Your word is a lamp to my feet and a light to my path" (Psalm 119:105, ASV).

3. **Exposing Sin:** God's moral laws act as a mirror, revealing our sin and need for a Savior. As Paul writes, "through the law comes knowledge of sin" (Romans 3:20, ESV).

4. **Pointing to Christ:** The moral laws point us to Christ, who fulfilled the law and offers us grace. As Paul explains, "Christ

is the end of the law for righteousness to everyone who believes" (Romans 10:4, ESV).

God's Moral Laws and Righteous Living

God's moral laws are indispensable for righteous living. They guide our actions, thoughts, and attitudes, aligning them with God's will. By obeying these laws, we reflect God's image, promote justice and love, and enhance our relationship with Him and others.

Righteous living doesn't mean mere external compliance with these laws but internal transformation—a heart conformed to the image of God. As Jesus emphasized, righteousness surpasses external legality, extending to the attitudes of the heart (Matthew 5:21-28, ESV).

God's Moral Laws and Grace

Understanding God's moral laws in light of His grace is critical. Our obedience to these laws doesn't earn salvation, which is a gift of God's grace through faith in Christ (Ephesians 2:8-9, ESV). These laws instead guide our response to this grace—a life of righteousness, gratitude, and love. As James explains, faith without works (obedience) is dead (James 2:17, ASV).

God's moral laws are a central part of His divine blueprint. They reveal His holy character, guide righteous living, expose our sin, and point us to Christ. As believers, obeying these laws doesn't secure our salvation but reflects our transformed heart. Thus, understanding and applying these laws is vital for a life that mirrors God's image and advances His kingdom. This understanding not only strengthens our relationship with God but also equips us to navigate the ethical challenges of our time. Therefore, the power of righteous living rooted in God's moral laws is invaluable in our Christian journey.

Chapter 8: Divine Intervention: God's Power in History

8.1 Egypt to Canaan: God's Power Over Nations

The historical narrative from Egypt to Canaan powerfully demonstrates God's sovereignty over nations and His ability to guide the course of events according to His divine plan.

God's Power in the Exodus

The Exodus story begins with the Israelites suffering under Egyptian slavery. God heard their cry and remembered His covenant with Abraham, Isaac, and Jacob (Exodus 2:24, ASV). In these dire circumstances, God unveiled His power, showing His dominance over Pharaoh and the false gods of Egypt.

The Ten Plagues were more than punitive; they were also polemic. They directly challenged the gods of Egypt, including Hapi (god of the Nile), Hathor (goddess of protection), Ra (sun god), and others. Each plague corresponded to an Egyptian deity, emphasizing the impotence of these false gods in the face of Jehovah's power (Exodus 7-12, ASV).

The climactic event was the Passover. God commanded the Israelites to slaughter a lamb and smear its blood on their doorposts. When Jehovah saw the blood, He "passed over" these houses, sparing them from the final plague—the death of the firstborn. This mighty act liberated the Israelites from slavery (Exodus 12:13, ASV).

God's Power at the Red Sea

The parting of the Red Sea was a monumental demonstration of God's power. As the Israelites stood between Pharaoh's approaching army and the Red Sea, Jehovah reassured them, "Fear ye not, stand still, and see the salvation of Jehovah, which he will work for you today" (Exodus 14:13, ASV). Jehovah then miraculously divided the sea, enabling the Israelites to cross on dry ground. When the Egyptians pursued, the waters returned, engulfing them. Through this event, God delivered His people and vanquished their enemies (Exodus 14:21-31, ASV).

God's Provision in the Wilderness

In the wilderness, Jehovah's power manifested through His providential care for Israel. Despite their grumblings, Jehovah graciously provided for their needs—manna for food, water from a rock, and protection from enemies. These miracles displayed Jehovah's power to sustain His people and His faithfulness to His covenant promises (Exodus 16-17, ASV).

God's Power in the Conquest of Canaan

Upon reaching Canaan, Jehovah's power was evident in the conquest of the land. From the miraculous crossing of the Jordan River to the fall of Jericho's walls, Jehovah demonstrated His power and fulfilled His promise to give Israel the land (Joshua 3-6, ASV).

The narrative from Egypt to Canaan is more than just history; it vividly demonstrates God's power and control over the nations. He hears the cries of the oppressed, delivers His people from their enemies, and guides them through trials and tribulations. Despite human plans and actions, God's purposes always prevail. This truth provides comfort and assurance in an uncertain world, reminding us of God's sovereign control over the course of history. As we submit to His Word and walk in His ways, we can experience His power in our lives, ensuring His continuous presence and guidance on our journey of faith.

8.2 The Fall of Babylon: God's Sovereignty

The Bible is a grand narrative that lays out the relationship between Jehovah God and the nations of the earth. This relationship is defined by divine interventions that make it abundantly clear that Jehovah is sovereign over the nations. A key episode that perfectly captures this truth is the fall of Babylon, as prophesied by the prophet Isaiah and chronicled by Daniel in the Old Testament.

Babylon was one of the most splendid cities of the ancient world, a center of trade, culture, and military power. Its fall was more than just a geopolitical event; it was a demonstration of God's sovereign power. When we examine the fall of Babylon, we're not merely delving into ancient history; we are observing the hand of God in the affairs of nations, affirming the truth that He is the "Lord of hosts, the God of Israel, who dwells above the cherubim" (Isaiah 37:16, ASV).

Prophetic Forewarnings

The book of Isaiah contains forewarnings of Babylon's fall. In Isaiah 13:19, the prophet declares, "And Babylon, the glory of kingdoms, the beauty of the Chaldees' pride, shall be as when God overthrew Sodom and Gomorrah" (ASV). This prophecy was given some 200 years before the fall of Babylon. It's a clear demonstration of God's foreknowledge (Note 5). Although God knew what would happen, He didn't determine the Babylonians' actions. They acted of their own volition, and their actions led to their fall.

The Writing on the Wall

Fast forward to Daniel 5, and we find King Belshazzar holding a great feast. As they drink from the sacred vessels taken from the temple in Jerusalem, a disembodied hand appears and writes a message on the wall. The words written – "MENE, MENE, TEKEL, UPHARSIN" – were a divine judgment upon Belshazzar and his kingdom. Daniel interprets this message, stating, "God has numbered the days of your kingdom and brought it to an end; you have been weighed in the balances and found wanting; your kingdom is divided and given to the Medes and Persians" (Daniel 5:26-28, ASV). That very night, the city was invaded, and Belshazzar was killed.

God's Sovereignty on Display

The fall of Babylon was not an accident of history. It was a fulfillment of prophecy and a demonstration of God's sovereignty. Babylon, despite its power and splendor, fell because it opposed God and His chosen people. The Babylonians had acted of their own free will, and their actions had consequences. But in these events, God's foreknowledge and sovereignty were on display. It served as a reminder to all nations that while humans have free will to make their choices, Jehovah is the supreme ruler, directing the course of history according to His divine plan and purpose.

In analyzing these events, it's crucial to remember that Babylon is more than just an ancient city. It symbolizes human societies and systems that exalt themselves against God. Throughout history, such societies have risen and fallen, proving the timeless truth that "Righteousness exalts a nation, but sin is a reproach to any people" (Proverbs 14:34, ASV).

The fall of Babylon also demonstrates the biblical principle of reaping what one sows. The Babylonians mistreated God's chosen people and misused the sacred vessels from the Jerusalem temple. In return, they experienced God's judgment. This principle continues to apply today; our actions have consequences, both in this life and the next.

Moreover, the fall of Babylon underscores the ultimate authority of Jehovah. Despite Babylon's earthly power, it could not withstand God's judgment. This truth holds a warning for all nations and individuals who might seek to oppose God. His will and purposes will always prevail, regardless of human plans or actions.

Conclusion: God's Sovereignty and Human Responsibility

The fall of Babylon is more than just a historical event. It's a powerful demonstration of God's sovereignty over the nations and a reminder of human responsibility. While God's sovereignty is absolute, it doesn't negate human responsibility. We have the free will to choose our actions, but we cannot escape the consequences of those actions, particularly when they are contrary to God's laws.

As we reflect on the fall of Babylon, we can glean important lessons about living in a world where God is sovereign. We should not be seduced by the allure of worldly power and success, for these are transient. Instead, our focus should be on obeying God and living according to His principles. Only by doing so can we hope to avoid the fate of Babylon and enjoy the blessings that come from living in harmony with God's will.

In this age, where secularism seeks to marginalize God's place in society, the fall of Babylon serves as a poignant reminder that Jehovah's sovereignty remains unchallenged. No matter how much humans may attempt to assert control, Jehovah, the creator of heaven and earth, is the one who "removes kings and sets up kings" (Daniel 2:21, ASV). His authority over the affairs of nations continues unabated, and His will shall ultimately prevail.

Thus, the fall of Babylon is not merely an ancient tale. It's an enduring testimony of God's sovereignty and a clarion call to recognize and submit to His rule. It also serves as a warning that, no matter how powerful or seemingly invincible, any kingdom that defies Jehovah God will ultimately fall. Just as ancient Babylon was judged, so too will any nation that lifts itself above God's rightful place. Let us, therefore, live in the light of this truth, ever mindful of Jehovah's sovereignty and our responsibility to live according to His Word.

8.3 Rise of Persia: God's Hand in Global Affairs

In the tapestry of history, there are numerous instances where the hand of Jehovah can be observed guiding global events. The rise of Persia, a significant milestone in ancient history, presents an extraordinary example of God's sovereignty in global affairs. As we dive into the annals of history and the biblical narratives, we can glean a profound understanding of the interplay between divine authority and human actions.

Cyrus the Great: God's Anointed

To appreciate the divine involvement in Persia's ascendancy, we must first turn our focus on Cyrus the Great, the founder of the Achaemenid Empire. In Isaiah 44:28, Jehovah declares, "Cyrus, he is my shepherd, and shall perform all my pleasure; even saying of Jerusalem, She shall be built; and of the temple, Thy foundation shall be laid" (ASV). Here, Jehovah proclaims Cyrus as his chosen instrument, centuries before his birth.

Furthermore, in Isaiah 45:1, Jehovah refers to Cyrus as His "anointed," stating, "Thus saith Jehovah to his anointed, to Cyrus, whose right hand I have holden…" (ASV). In the biblical context, to be anointed meant to be chosen by God for a specific task. Cyrus, despite not being an Israelite, was chosen by Jehovah to accomplish a significant mission, demonstrating God's sovereignty over all nations and rulers.

Persia's Role in God's Plan

The rise of Persia under Cyrus played a pivotal role in the unfolding of God's divine plan. Persia, emerging as a world power, conquered Babylon in 539 B.C.E. thereby fulfilling the prophecies about Babylon's fall. Cyrus's decree allowing the Jews to return to their homeland and rebuild their temple (Ezra 1:1-4, ASV) was a crucial step in fulfilling the divine will.

This decree was a fulfillment of Jeremiah's prophecy that after 70 years of exile, the Jews would return to their homeland (Jeremiah 29:10, ASV). It was Jehovah's sovereignty that moved Cyrus to issue this decree, evidence of God's active role in global affairs.

God's Sovereignty and Human Free Will

The story of Cyrus and the rise of Persia provides a fascinating study of the interaction between God's sovereignty and human free will. Jehovah had foreknowledge of Cyrus's actions and the rise of Persia (Note 5). Yet, He did not dictate Cyrus's decisions. As a free moral agent, Cyrus made his choices, but these were known by God beforehand.

Jehovah's foreknowledge of these events does not undermine human free will, rather it showcases His omniscience and ultimate control over the course of history. He can foresee events and outcomes, yet without coercing human decisions. This delicate balance between God's sovereign control and human freedom is a testament to His supreme wisdom and power.

Reflections on the Rise of Persia

The rise of Persia serves as a powerful reminder of God's omnipotence and His active involvement in human history. It is evidence that even the mightiest empires are subject to His authority. In the grand scheme of history, it is not the strength of armies or the cunning of kings that ultimately determines the course of nations. Rather, it is the hand of God, guiding and steering events towards His divine purposes.

Furthermore, the rise of Persia reaffirms that God's promises are certain. The prophecies concerning Babylon's fall and Israel's restoration were fulfilled precisely. It underscores the veracity of the biblical record and its prophetic reliability, asserting that the Bible is the inspired, inerrant Word of God (Note 6).

Conclusion: Divine Intervention and Global Affairs

The rise of Persia and the role of Cyrus the Great in the fulfillment of divine prophecy demonstrate Jehovah's power to intervene in human history, even in the realm of global affairs. He is not a distant observer but an active participant, steering events towards His predetermined plans.

In a world where secular ideologies often push God to the margins, this biblical account serves as a reminder of His active role and supreme authority. Regardless of human machinations, His will prevails. As we study and reflect upon these events, we gain a profound understanding of God's sovereignty and His enduring influence in global affairs.

In conclusion, the rise of Persia is a powerful testament to God's hand in global affairs. It is a potent reminder that Jehovah's sovereignty transcends human politics and powers. No nation, no king, no empire can resist His will or thwart His plans. As we traverse the corridors of history, we see the indelible imprint of His sovereignty, underscoring the eternal truth that "the Most High rules the kingdom of men and gives it to whom he will" (Daniel 4:32, ESV).

8.4 The Arrival of the Messiah: Fulfillment of Prophecy

In the grand narrative of human history, the arrival of the Messiah stands as a pivotal moment of divine intervention, underscoring Jehovah's active role in the course of human events. This crucial incident epitomizes the fulfillment of prophecy and affirms God's omnipotent power and unwavering faithfulness to His promises.

The Prophetic Foretelling of the Messiah

Numerous prophecies in the Old Testament pointed towards the coming of the Messiah, the Anointed One. The prophets, inspired by the Holy Spirit, laid out specific markers that would characterize His coming. For instance, Isaiah prophesied that a virgin would conceive and bear a son named Immanuel (Isaiah 7:14, ASV). Further, Micah stated that the Messiah would be born in Bethlehem (Micah 5:2, ASV). These prophetic utterances, among others, were fulfilled in the life of Jesus Christ, validating His messianic identity.

Jesus Christ: The Fulfillment of Prophecy

The life of Jesus Christ fulfilled the Old Testament prophecies in meticulous detail. His birth to a virgin in Bethlehem (Matthew 1:18-25, ESV), His teachings and miracles, His sacrificial death, and His resurrection all align with the prophetic narrative of the Old Testament. This precision in the fulfillment of prophecy underscores the inerrant nature of the Holy Scriptures (Note 6) and illuminates the divine orchestration behind the scenes of human history.

Even in His death, Jesus fulfilled prophecy. Consider Psalm 22:16-18, "For dogs have compassed me: A company of evil-doers have inclosed me; They pierced my hands and my feet. I may count all my bones. They look and stare upon me. They part my garments among them, And upon my vesture do they cast lots" (ASV). These verses foreshadow the crucifixion of Jesus (Matthew 27:35, ESV).

Divine Sovereignty and Human Freedom

The fulfillment of messianic prophecy provides a rich illustration of the balance between divine sovereignty and human free will (Note 5). While Jehovah had perfect foreknowledge of the events surrounding the arrival of the Messiah, He did not coerce human decisions to ensure the fulfillment of prophecy. Instead, human actions - even those that led to the crucifixion of Christ - were the product of individual free will, which God knew in advance and incorporated into His divine plan.

The Significance of the Messiah's Arrival

The arrival of the Messiah served a transformative role in human history and salvific plan of God. Jesus, through His teachings and sacrificial death, paved the way for the redemption of humanity from sin. This intervention ushered in a new covenant, distinct from the Mosaic Law, based on faith in Christ (Romans 10:4, ESV). The spiritual principles of the Mosaic Law, however, remain applicable to Christians, reminding them of their moral obligations (Note 8).

Conclusion: The Arrival of the Messiah and Divine Intervention

The arrival of the Messiah, as prophesied in the Old Testament and fulfilled in the life of Jesus Christ, stands as a testament to God's divine intervention in human history. This historic event demonstrates the intricate interplay of divine sovereignty and human free will, as God's foreknowledge of events does not compromise the freedom of human decision-making.

The fulfillment of prophecy in the coming of the Messiah affirms the veracity and inerrancy of the Holy Scriptures, emphasizing their reliability as the Word of God. Furthermore, this fulfillment manifests God's faithfulness to His promises, underscoring His unchanging nature and commitment to His divine plan.

Thus, the arrival of the Messiah serves as a beacon of hope and salvation, a testament to God's love for humanity, and a powerful illustration of His divine intervention in human history. It stands as an enduring reminder that God's will prevails, His Word is trustworthy, and His promises are unfailing. Even amidst the intricacies of human affairs, His divine purposes are ultimately fulfilled.

8.5 The Early Church: God's Power in Persecution

The growth and establishment of the early church, against all odds, is a significant testament to the reality of divine intervention in human history. Despite extreme persecution, the Christian faith not only survived but thrived, signaling the power and providence of God working in the world.

Persecution in the Early Church

The early Christians were subjected to severe persecution, especially in the Roman Empire, during the 1st and 2nd centuries C.E. Their refusal to worship the Roman gods and emperors made them subjects of ridicule, discrimination, and brutal violence. The Book of Acts chronicles several instances of this persecution, such as the stoning of Stephen (Acts 7:54-60, ESV) and the widespread persecution following Stephen's death (Acts 8:1, ESV).

Divine Intervention Amid Persecution

In the face of severe trials, the early Christians drew strength from their faith in Christ and the guidance of the Holy Spirit-inspired words (Note 4). Despite their human frailties, the apostles and early disciples demonstrated remarkable courage and resilience that can only be attributed to divine intervention.

Consider the transformation of the Apostle Peter, who, out of fear, denied Jesus three times before His crucifixion (Matthew 26:69-75, ESV). Yet, this same Peter became a bold and unwavering leader in the early church, fearlessly proclaiming the Gospel even in the face of imprisonment and death threats (Acts 4:5-12, ESV). Such a radical transformation underscores the divine power at work within the early church.

The Spread of the Gospel

Despite intense opposition, the Gospel message spread rapidly throughout the Roman Empire and beyond. This growth can be attributed to the divine hand guiding the missionary efforts of the early Christians. The Apostle Paul, formerly a staunch persecutor of Christians, became a passionate evangelist, establishing churches in various cities across the Roman Empire (Acts 13-28, ESV).

Paul's conversion on the Damascus road (Acts 9:1-19, ESV) can only be understood as a divine intervention that completely redirected his life's course. He affirmed that the Gospel he preached was not his own, but a revelation from Jesus Christ (Galatians 1:11-12, ESV). God's hand was undoubtedly at work, even in the midst of severe persecution, to ensure the propagation of the Gospel.

Perseverance Amid Trials

The early church's perseverance amid trials is a demonstration of divine intervention. The Apostle James encouraged the early Christians to consider trials as pure joy because the testing of faith produces perseverance (James 1:2-4, ESV). This attitude, shaped by divine wisdom and perspective, enabled the early church to endure and grow amid persecution.

The Growth of the Early Church: God's Providence at Work

The growth and survival of the early church amid persecution serve as potent evidence of God's providence and power. Despite the formidable challenges, the early Christians remained steadfast, committed to their faith and spurred on by divine strength.

The Holy Spirit-inspired words served as their guide and source of encouragement. The believers gathered together for the teaching of the apostles, for fellowship, breaking of bread, and for prayers (Acts 2:42, ESV), demonstrating their reliance on the Word of God and the power of communal prayer.

Conclusion: Divine Power in the Midst of Persecution

In conclusion, the story of the early church and its growth amid severe persecution is a powerful testimony of divine intervention in history. God's providence and power were manifestly evident in the transformation of the apostles, the rapid spread of the Gospel, and the perseverance of the early Christians.

The divine hand at work in the early church offers Christians today the assurance that God remains at work in the world, advancing His divine purposes even amid trials and tribulations. Despite persecution, the Word of God endures and accomplishes the purpose for which it was sent (Isaiah 55:11, ASV), affirming the invincibility of divine truth and the unstoppable progress of God's kingdom.

8.6 Modern-Day Spiritual Israel: God's Power in Restoration

God's power of restoration continues to be made manifest in what can be termed as modern-day Spiritual Israel, represented by the body of Christian believers. It's vital to note that according to the teachings of Jesus, this "Spiritual Israel" isn't an exclusive reference to the Jewish people. Instead, it pertains to all those who accept Christ and bear the fruits of the kingdom of God (Matthew 21:43, ESV).

Spiritual Israel: A New Identity

The Apostle Paul affirmed this concept, stating that not all descendants of Israel belong to Israel and not all are children of Abraham because they are his offspring (Romans 9:6-8, ESV). Rather, "it is not the children of the flesh who are the children of God, but the children of the promise are counted as offspring" (Romans 9:8, ESV). This indicates a shift from physical ancestry to spiritual lineage as the criteria for being God's chosen people.

This new Spiritual Israel is not confined by ethnicity or nationality but is instead characterized by faith in Christ. Paul states that in Christ, "there is neither Jew nor Greek, slave nor free, male nor female, for you are all one in Christ Jesus" (Galatians 3:28, ESV). These words underscore the universality of the new covenant in Christ, open to all who believe, thereby creating a new Spiritual Israel.

God's Power in Spiritual Restoration

God's power in restoration is evident in the manner He draws individuals from all nations and backgrounds into the body of Christ. Through the Holy Spirit-inspired Word, individuals are spiritually restored, redeemed, and reconciled to God through faith in Christ (2

Corinthians 5:17-19, ESV). This process marks a transition from spiritual death to life, indicative of God's transformative power in restoration.

This transformation is not limited to an individual's relationship with God but extends to their relationships with others. The Apostle Paul, in his letters, frequently emphasizes the importance of unity, forgiveness, and love among believers, all of which exemplify the power of God in restoring broken relationships and fostering a sense of community within the body of Christ.

Sustaining Spiritual Israel

Spiritual Israel, while not exempt from trials and tribulations, is sustained and nourished by God's power. As the Apostle Peter notes, believers are shielded by God's power until the coming of the salvation to be revealed in the last time (1 Peter 1:5, ESV). This divine sustenance is also evident in the gift of the Holy Spirit-inspired Word that guides and directs believers in their spiritual journey.

Spiritual Israel and the Kingdom of God

The emergence and growth of Spiritual Israel signify the expansion of God's kingdom on earth. While the physical nation of Israel in the Old Testament was central to God's plan at that time, the arrival of Christ marked a new era where the kingdom of God is not tied to a particular ethnic group or geographic location, but instead extends to all who accept Christ and seek to follow His teachings.

Conclusion: A Continual Process

In conclusion, the concept of modern-day Spiritual Israel encapsulates the transformative and restorative power of God at work in human history. Through faith in Christ, individuals from diverse backgrounds are united into a spiritual body, marking a significant shift from physical to spiritual lineage as the defining factor of God's chosen people.

This transition has not been a one-time event, but a continual process, indicative of God's active role in human history. As believers strive to live in accordance with Christ's teachings, they partake in the expansion of God's kingdom on earth, attesting to the ongoing power of God's divine intervention in history.

Chapter 9: Walking in Wisdom: God's Power in Discernment

9.1 Solomon's Wisdom: A Gift from Above

The Bible vividly depicts the wisdom of Solomon, presenting him as an exemplar of divine wisdom. The account of Solomon's wisdom, its origin, and its application, vividly illustrates the power of God in gifting and shaping discernment.

The Source of Solomon's Wisdom

It's clear in the Bible that Solomon's wisdom was a divine endowment, a gift from God. Solomon became king after his father, David, and was keenly aware of the responsibilities his new role entailed. In a dream, Jehovah appeared to Solomon and said, "Ask what I shall give thee" (1 Kings 3:5, ASV). Solomon requested an understanding heart to judge God's people, to discern between good and evil. God was pleased with this request and granted him a wise and discerning heart, saying there had never been anyone like him, nor would there ever be (1 Kings 3:12, ASV).

Manifestation of Solomon's Wisdom

The manifestation of Solomon's wisdom is perhaps most notably demonstrated in his judgment between two women both claiming to be the mother of the same baby. Solomon's proposed solution - to divide the child in two, allowed the real mother's compassionate plea to reveal the truth (1 Kings 3:16-28, ASV). This story affirms the extraordinary wisdom Solomon possessed.

Moreover, Solomon's wisdom extended beyond adjudicating disputes. It played a crucial role in governance, diplomacy, poetry, and natural sciences. People from all nations, including the Queen of Sheba, came to listen to his wisdom (1 Kings 4:34, ASV; 10:1-13, ASV).

Wisdom in Solomon's Writings

Solomon's wisdom is also evident in his writings, namely Proverbs, Ecclesiastes, and Song of Solomon. These books offer deep insights on various aspects of life, morality, and the pursuit of a meaningful existence. Proverbs, in particular, is replete with wise sayings and practical instructions on living righteously, further solidifying Solomon's reputation as a wise king.

Wisdom: A Reflection of God's Character

The wisdom of Solomon underscores the importance of wisdom as a divine attribute. The Bible teaches that the fear of Jehovah is the beginning of wisdom (Proverbs 9:10, ASV), suggesting that true wisdom begins with acknowledging and revering God. Wisdom, thus, is not simply intellectual or practical skill but is deeply connected with moral and spiritual understanding.

The Fall of Solomon: A Cautionary Tale

However, Solomon's story also serves as a cautionary tale about the proper use of wisdom. Despite his wisdom, Solomon allowed foreign wives to turn his heart after other gods, leading to idolatry (1 Kings 11:1-8, ASV). This part of Solomon's story underscores that wisdom should not be isolated from obedience to God.

Solomon's Wisdom: A Foreshadowing of Christ

In the New Testament, Jesus refers to Solomon's wisdom while emphasizing His greater significance: "The queen of the South...came from the ends of the earth to hear the wisdom of Solomon, and behold, something greater than Solomon is here" (Matthew 12:42,

ESV). In this context, Solomon's wisdom not only serves as an example of divine blessing but also foreshadows the superior wisdom found in Christ.

The story of Solomon's wisdom offers rich insights into the nature of wisdom as a divine gift, reflecting God's character and His willingness to endow His servants with the ability to discern good from evil, administer justice, and guide people in righteousness. It illustrates that true wisdom is not a mere human attribute but a divine endowment, aligning with God's moral order. The life of Solomon warns of the consequences when wisdom is misused, underlining the importance of faithfulness to God.

The essence of Solomon's wisdom – discernment, justice, prudence, and fear of God - continues to instruct believers today, encouraging them to seek wisdom from God and apply it in their lives, as Solomon did in his best times. Solomon's wisdom, thus, is a testament to God's power in bestowing discernment, a precious gift to navigate the complexities of life in a manner pleasing to God.

9.2 Discerning Good from Evil: God's Power in Moral Judgments

Discernment, the ability to judge well, is a necessary attribute for the faithful follower of God. More specifically, the ability to discern good from evil is crucial in maintaining a righteous and godly life. As demonstrated throughout the Bible, discernment comes from understanding and applying God's Word.

The Origin of Discernment

According to the Bible, true discernment comes from God and is deeply tied to wisdom, understanding, and knowledge, which all stem from Him. Proverbs 2:6, ASV states, "For Jehovah giveth wisdom; Out of his mouth cometh knowledge and understanding." It follows that discernment, as a component of wisdom, is derived from God and is available to those who seek it in earnest.

God's Word as the Guide

The primary tool for developing discernment is the Word of God. By studying and meditating upon the Scriptures, believers equip themselves to make moral judgments aligned with God's standards. The author of Hebrews states, "For the word of God is living and active, sharper than any two-edged sword, piercing to the division of soul and of spirit, of joints and of marrow, and discerning the thoughts and intentions of the heart" (Hebrews 4:12, ESV). The Bible serves as the standard for discerning good from evil, providing a moral framework to guide believers' actions and decisions.

Discernment in Action: The Early Church

In the early Church, discernment was necessary to understand and apply the teachings of Christ correctly. The apostle Paul prayed for the Philippians, "that your love may abound more and more, with knowledge and all discernment, so that you may approve what is excellent, and so be pure and blameless for the day of Christ" (Philippians 1:9-10, ESV). This prayer highlights the importance of discernment in maintaining purity and righteousness.

Discernment and Free Will

However, the possession of discernment does not negate human free will. Individuals are free to choose whether to follow God's standards or not. Even Solomon, endowed with divine wisdom and discernment, made unwise choices that led him away from God. This freedom to choose underscores the significance of actively seeking discernment and applying it correctly in making moral judgments.

Discernment in a Fallen World

In our modern world, discernment is increasingly necessary to navigate the complexities of life. The moral and ethical landscape today presents many gray areas that require careful discernment based on God's Word. As the apostle John advised, "Beloved, do not believe every spirit, but test the spirits to see whether they are from God, for many false prophets have gone out into the world" (1 John 4:1, ESV). In a world fraught with spiritual deception, discernment is a necessary guard against falsehood.

Discernment as a Process

The development of discernment is a continuous process. It involves regular engagement with the Scriptures, prayer, and practical application of God's Word. This process is not automatic but requires commitment, effort, and a sincere desire to live according to God's standards. As believers grow in their understanding of God's Word, they also grow in discernment.

Discerning good from evil is a critical aspect of living a life pleasing to God. God's power in moral judgments, made manifest in the divine wisdom and understanding that flow from His Word, equips believers with discernment. This discernment, diligently sought and correctly applied, enables believers to navigate the complexities of life in alignment with God's will. Despite the challenges of our fallen world, God's Word offers clear, unchanging standards for discernment, serving as a reliable guide in all situations. Therefore, believers must continually seek wisdom and understanding from God, studying His Word and applying it in their lives, to develop the discernment necessary to judge rightly and live faithfully.

9.3 The Wisdom in Proverbs: God's Power for Daily Living

The book of Proverbs, located in the heart of the Bible, is an invaluable source of divine wisdom that enables believers to navigate daily life in alignment with God's will. These powerful, concise statements of truth offer practical guidance, godly insight, and discernment for dealing with various aspects of human life – relationships, speech, work, morality, and the stewardship of resources, among others.

The Purpose of Proverbs

The Proverbs were not merely written as a guide for ethical conduct or a manual for good behavior. Instead, their purpose is far more profound. The book of Proverbs seeks to impart wisdom and understanding to its readers and instruct them in the ways of righteousness, justice, and equity (Proverbs 1:2-3, ASV). This wisdom, when rightly applied, empowers believers to live a life that pleases Jehovah and benefits themselves and their communities.

The Fear of Jehovah: The Beginning of Wisdom

Central to the wisdom imparted in Proverbs is the concept of the fear of Jehovah. Proverbs 1:7, ASV states, "The fear of Jehovah is the beginning of knowledge; but the foolish despise wisdom and instruction." This fear is not one of terror or dread but rather a reverent awe and deep respect for God and His ways. It involves a recognition of His sovereignty, a commitment to obey His commands, and a desire to honor Him in all aspects of life. This foundational attitude is the starting point for gaining true wisdom and discernment.

Wisdom for Relationships

One of the primary areas where Proverbs provides wisdom is in relationships. Whether dealing with family dynamics, friendships, or interactions with neighbors and strangers, Proverbs offers principles that guide interactions and promote harmony. For instance, the book emphasizes the value of honesty, kindness, patience, and peacefulness in dealing with others (Proverbs 14:21; 15:1; 16:24; 25:21-22, ASV).

Wisdom for Speech

The words we speak can bring life or death, and the book of Proverbs gives significant attention to this aspect. It cautions against rash words, lying, gossip, and contentious speech, while advocating for truth, gentleness, and timely, appropriate words (Proverbs 12:18; 15:4;

16:24; 18:21, ASV). The wisdom contained in Proverbs guides believers to use their speech to build up rather than tear down.

Wisdom for Work

Proverbs also provides guidance on work and diligence. It warns against laziness and promotes diligence, planning, and integrity in work (Proverbs 6:6-11; 12:11; 13:4; 21:5, ASV). The book advocates for a balanced view of work, one that acknowledges the blessings of diligent labor but also recognizes the dangers of overwork and the pursuit of riches at the expense of righteousness.

Wisdom in Stewardship

The wise management of resources, including time, talents, and wealth, is another area where Proverbs offers invaluable guidance. It promotes generosity, cautions against greed, and encourages prudent financial practices (Proverbs 3:9-10; 11:24-25; 13:11; 21:20, ASV). The wisdom of Proverbs thus empowers believers to be faithful stewards of God-given resources.

The wisdom found in Proverbs is timeless and universally applicable, providing believers with divine guidance for daily living. However, it is not enough merely to read or memorize these proverbs. True wisdom, as underscored throughout the book, involves the application of these truths in daily life. Only then can believers experience the full benefit of this divine wisdom and embody the discernment God desires.

Yet, as we apply these truths, it is vital to remember that human effort alone cannot attain wisdom. Divine wisdom is ultimately a gift from God, a product of His grace and mercy. As we seek wisdom from God and immerse ourselves in His Word, we can confidently navigate the complexities of life, guided by the infallible wisdom of our Creator. As Proverbs 2:6, ASV states, "For Jehovah giveth wisdom; out of His mouth cometh knowledge and understanding."

9.4 Discerning God's Will: The Power of Divine Guidance

Discerning God's will is an essential aspect of a believer's walk of faith. It involves understanding and aligning oneself with God's divine plans and purposes as revealed in His Word. With the Holy Spirit-inspired words serving as our guide, we can accurately perceive and apply God's will in our lives, leading to a life filled with purpose, joy, and fulfillment.

Understanding God's Will

God's will, as revealed in the Bible, is His purposeful direction for creation and His desire for humanity. His will encompasses His plans for salvation, His moral standards, and His specific guidance for individuals' lives. The Bible provides a comprehensive outline of God's will, with God's purpose being primarily to glorify Himself and reconcile humanity to Himself through Jesus Christ (Ephesians 1:11-12, ESV).

God's Moral Will

God's moral will comprises His commandments and principles regarding right and wrong. It is His standard for human behavior, reflecting His perfect character and righteous standards. This aspect of God's will is unchanging and universal, applicable to all people, regardless of time or culture. The Ten Commandments, the teachings of Jesus, and the ethical guidelines found in the Epistles are all aspects of God's moral will (Exodus 20:1-17, ASV; Matthew 22:37-39; Romans 12:9-21, ESV).

God's Sovereign Will

God's sovereign will encompasses His ultimate plans for the universe, which He carries out according to His wisdom and power. This aspect of God's will is often unseen and unknown by humans until it unfolds. While His sovereign will can be challenging to comprehend, believers can trust that God works all things for good for those who love Him and are called according to His purpose (Romans 8:28, ESV).

God's Individual Will

God's individual will involves His specific guidance for each person's life. While not every decision or situation is explicitly addressed in Scripture, the Bible provides principles that can guide decisions, and believers are encouraged to seek wisdom through prayer and counsel when discerning God's individual will (James 1:5; Proverbs 3:5-6; 11:14, ESV).

The Role of Wisdom and the Word of God

Wisdom plays a critical role in discerning God's will. Proverbs 2:6, ASV states, "For Jehovah giveth wisdom; out of His mouth cometh knowledge and understanding." This wisdom is attained through a diligent study of the Word of God, prayer, and the counsel of godly individuals. As we grow in wisdom, we become better equipped to understand and apply God's will in our lives.

The Word of God is our primary source for understanding God's will. Through studying Scripture, we gain insights into God's character, His purposes, and His standards. The Holy Spirit-inspired words serve as a lamp to our feet and a light to our path, guiding us in the ways of righteousness (Psalm 119:105, ASV).

Prayer and Godly Counsel

Prayer is a critical element in discerning God's will. Through prayer, we communicate with God, express our desires, and seek His guidance. James 1:5, ESV assures us that if we lack wisdom, we should ask God, who gives generously to all without reproach, and it will be given to us.

In addition, godly counsel can provide valuable insight when discerning God's will. Proverbs 11:14, ESV advises that where there is no guidance, a people falls, but in an abundance of counselors there is safety. By consulting with mature believers who are well-versed in the Scriptures, we can gain wisdom and clarity.

Walking in Obedience

Discerning God's will involves more than merely understanding it; it requires obedience. As we align our lives with God's will and walk in obedience to His commands, we experience the fullness of His blessings and purpose for our lives. Deuteronomy 10:12-13, ASV illustrates this, stating, "And now, Israel, what doth Jehovah thy God require of thee, but to fear Jehovah thy God, to walk in all his ways, and to love him, and to serve Jehovah thy God with all thy heart and with all thy soul, to keep the commandments of Jehovah, and his statutes, which I command thee this day for thy good?"

Discerning God's will is a journey that involves diligent study of the Scriptures, fervent prayer, wise counsel, and obedient action. By seeking God's will in all aspects of our lives, we can walk in wisdom, experience His divine guidance, and fulfill the purpose He has ordained for us. We can trust that His will is perfect, aligning with His character and purposes, and always aiming towards the ultimate good of His creation and glory of His name. In the words of Romans 12:2, ESV, "Do not be conformed to this world, but be transformed by the renewal of your mind, that by testing you may discern what is the will of God, what is good and acceptable and perfect."

9.5 Wisdom in Suffering: The Power of God in Trials

Life is a journey filled with ebbs and flows, joy and suffering. As Christians, we often face trials that test our faith, patience, and endurance. However, in the midst of these trials, there is an opportunity for wisdom and growth, and the power of God can be profoundly experienced.

Understanding Suffering

Suffering is an unavoidable aspect of human existence. While some may question why a loving God would permit suffering, the Bible makes it clear that suffering is not a punishment from God but rather a consequence of living in a fallen world. It's important to understand that God did not design suffering; rather, it is a result of humanity's disobedience in the Garden of Eden (Genesis 3:17-19, ASV).

However, God, in His infinite wisdom and power, can use suffering for our good and His glory. Romans 5:3-5, ESV, states, "Not only that, but we rejoice in our sufferings, knowing that suffering produces endurance, and endurance produces character, and character produces hope, and hope does not put us to shame, because God's love has been poured into our hearts through the Holy Spirit who has been given to us."

The Purpose of Trials

Trials, though painful, serve multiple purposes in the life of a believer. One primary purpose is refining our faith. Just as gold is refined through fire, our faith is tested and purified through trials (1 Peter 1:6-7, ESV).

Additionally, trials can bring us closer to God, fostering a deeper reliance on His strength rather than our own. When we face suffering, we are often driven to seek God's face more fervently, which leads to a more intimate relationship with Him (James 4:8, ESV).

Finally, trials can develop our character and cultivate virtues such as patience, endurance, and humility. These virtues are essential for Christian maturity and effective service in God's kingdom (James 1:2-4, ESV).

The Power of God in Trials

In our trials, we are not left powerless or without hope. The power of God is abundantly available to us, providing strength, comfort, and guidance amidst the storm.

God's power in our trials is evident in several ways. Firstly, He provides comfort in our suffering. As 2 Corinthians 1:3-4, ESV states, "Blessed be the God and Father of our Lord Jesus Christ, the Father of mercies and God of all comfort, who comforts us in all our affliction, so that we may be able to comfort those who are in any affliction, with the comfort with which we ourselves are comforted by God."

Secondly, God gives us strength in our weakness. When we acknowledge our insufficiency and lean on His omnipotence, His power is made perfect in us. This is beautifully illustrated in 2 Corinthians 12:9-10, ESV, "But he said to me, 'My grace is sufficient for you, for my power is made perfect in weakness.' Therefore I will boast all the more gladly of my weaknesses, so that the power of Christ may rest upon me."

Lastly, God provides wisdom in our trials. James 1:5, ESV, promises that "If any of you lacks wisdom, let him ask God, who gives generously to all without reproach, and it will be given him." When we seek wisdom from God, He provides divine perspective and guidance, helping us navigate our trials effectively.

The Role of Prayer and the Word of God

In trials, prayer and the Word of God are our primary resources. Through prayer, we communicate with God, expressing our fears, frustrations, and needs, while also seeking His wisdom and strength. In His Word, we find comfort, guidance, encouragement, and hope. Regular engagement with Scripture and prayer equips us to face trials with godly wisdom and resilience.

Suffering and trials are challenging aspects of our Christian journey, yet they offer unique opportunities for growth, transformation, and the manifestation of God's power. As we seek God's wisdom in suffering, we learn to navigate our trials with faith and endurance, drawing closer to Him and growing in Christian maturity. Remember the words of Romans 8:18, ESV, "For I consider that the sufferings of this present time are not worth comparing with the glory that is to be revealed to us." In our trials, we can look forward to the promise of future glory, confident in God's unfailing love and power.

9.6 The Wisdom of Christ: God's Power for Redemption

The wisdom of Christ, displayed through His teachings, His sacrificial death, and His victorious resurrection, is the power source for our redemption. The redemption plan orchestrated by God required the profound wisdom of Christ, which transcends human understanding, to fulfill the complex requirements of divine justice and mercy.

The Wisdom of Christ: His Teachings and Actions

The wisdom of Christ is vividly depicted in His teachings and actions. His parables, for example, were filled with spiritual insight and practical wisdom, providing profound truths about God, human nature, and the Kingdom of Heaven. The Parable of the Prodigal Son (Luke 15:11-32, ESV), for instance, reveals God's abundant grace and mercy towards repentant sinners.

Moreover, Jesus' actions demonstrated His wisdom. He healed the sick, forgave sinners, and confronted religious hypocrisy, demonstrating the heart of God's law—love and mercy. His ultimate action, the willingness to die on the cross for our sins, was the pinnacle of divine wisdom, a paradox to those who do not understand God's love (1 Corinthians 1:18, ESV).

The Wisdom of Christ: The Power for Redemption

The sacrificial death and resurrection of Jesus Christ is the embodiment of divine wisdom. Through these acts, Christ fulfilled the law, appeased divine justice, conquered death, and opened the way for humanity's redemption. The apostle Paul refers to this mystery of redemption through Christ as the "hidden wisdom" of God, which He predestined for our glory (1 Corinthians 2:7-8, ESV).

Through His death, Jesus Christ satisfied the divine requirement for justice. He bore the punishment for our sins, offering Himself as a sinless sacrifice, thereby appeasing the wrath of God (Isaiah 53:5-6, ASV). This act of self-sacrifice was a profound demonstration of divine wisdom, reconciling God's justice with His mercy.

The resurrection of Christ was equally instrumental in our redemption. Through His victory over death, Jesus Christ broke the power of sin and death, guaranteeing eternal life to all who believe in Him (1 Corinthians 15:54-57, ESV). This incredible act of divine wisdom secured our redemption and instilled hope for a glorious eternal future.

Applying the Wisdom of Christ

Understanding the wisdom of Christ in our redemption is essential for our Christian journey. It influences our perception of God, ourselves, and our world. It also shapes our response to God's offer of salvation and our interaction with others.

By recognizing our sinfulness and the severity of our spiritual condition, we can appreciate the need for Christ's redeeming work and gratefully accept His offer of salvation (Romans 3:23-24, ESV). We also understand that our salvation is not a result of our works or righteousness, but entirely the result of Christ's sacrifice and God's grace (Ephesians 2:8-9, ESV).

Moreover, understanding the wisdom of Christ prompts us to live lives worthy of our calling, reflecting Christ's love, forgiveness, and humility in our interactions with others (Philippians 2:1-5, ESV). It motivates us to share the good news of redemption with others, so they too can experience the power of Christ's wisdom and the joy of salvation.

The wisdom of Christ is the foundation of our redemption. His teachings, His sacrificial death, and His victorious resurrection reveal the profound wisdom of God, providing a way for humanity to be redeemed and reconciled to Him. As we strive to understand and apply this wisdom, we are empowered to live as redeemed people, reflecting Christ's love and grace in our lives and sharing the hope of redemption with others. As stated in 1 Corinthians 1:30, ESV, "And because of Him you are in Christ Jesus, who became to us wisdom from God, righteousness and sanctification and redemption." Christ's wisdom, therefore, is not just theoretical knowledge; it is transformative power for redemption.

Chapter 10: Eternal Promises: God's Power in Salvation

10.1 The Promise of the Messiah: A Display of Redemptive Power

The promise of the Messiah is a core theme in both the Old and New Testaments, revealing God's redemptive plan for humankind. This promise is not merely a prophetic announcement, but a display of God's redemptive power, which culminates in the person and work of Jesus Christ.

Promise of the Messiah in the Old Testament

The promise of a Messiah, a divinely appointed redeemer, can be traced back to the book of Genesis. Following the Fall, God declared to the serpent, "I will put enmity between thee and the woman, and between thy seed and her seed: he shall bruise thy head, and thou shalt bruise his heel" (Genesis 3:15, ASV). This protoevangelium, or first gospel, foreshadows the Messiah who would decisively crush the power of evil.

The Messianic promise unfolds progressively throughout the Old Testament. In the Abrahamic Covenant, God promises that through Abraham's offspring all nations on earth would be blessed (Genesis 12:3, ASV), a prophecy that ultimately points to Christ (Galatians 3:16, ESV). Later, the Davidic Covenant promises a king from David's line who would establish an everlasting kingdom (2 Samuel 7:12-16, ASV), fulfilled in Jesus, the eternal King (Luke 1:32-33, ESV).

The prophets also spoke about the coming Messiah. Isaiah, for example, foretold the coming of a suffering servant who would bear our iniquities and bring us peace (Isaiah 53:5, ASV), a prophecy explicitly fulfilled in Christ's atoning death (1 Peter 2:24, ESV).

THE POWER OF GOD

Promise of the Messiah in the New Testament

The New Testament opens with the fulfillment of the Messianic promise. Matthew's Gospel begins with the genealogy of Jesus, tracing His lineage back to Abraham and David, thereby linking Him to the Old Testament covenants (Matthew 1:1-17, ESV). Furthermore, the angelic announcement of Jesus' birth to Mary highlights His Messianic identity, declaring that "He will be great and will be called the Son of the Most High. And the Lord God will give to him the throne of his father David" (Luke 1:32, ESV).

The life, death, and resurrection of Jesus Christ bear witness to the fulfillment of the Messianic promise. Jesus Himself testified to His Messianic identity, declaring, "The Spirit of the Lord is upon me, because he has anointed me to proclaim good news to the poor. He has sent me to proclaim liberty to the captives and recovering of sight to the blind, to set at liberty those who are oppressed" (Luke 4:18, ESV).

Moreover, the apostles preached Christ as the promised Messiah. Peter, in his Pentecost sermon, proclaimed Jesus as both Lord and Christ (Acts 2:36, ESV). Paul, too, preached "Jesus is the Christ" (Acts 9:22, ESV), emphasizing that He fulfilled the promises made to the patriarchs (Romans 15:8, ESV).

The Redemptive Power of the Messiah

The promise of the Messiah displays God's redemptive power. In Christ, God provided the ultimate solution to humanity's sin problem. Through His sacrificial death, Christ bore the penalty of our sins, thereby satisfying God's justice (Romans 3:25-26, ESV). Furthermore, His resurrection broke the power of sin and death, guaranteeing eternal life to all who trust in Him (1 Corinthians 15:20-22, ESV).

This redemptive power is not limited to personal salvation. The coming of the Messiah ushered in the Kingdom of God, a realm where God's rule is acknowledged, and His will is done. In this Kingdom, God is redeeming not just individuals but all of creation (Romans 8:19-23, ESV).

In conclusion, the promise of the Messiah showcases God's redemptive power in history, culminating in the person and work of Jesus Christ. It is a promise rooted in the Old Testament, fulfilled in the New Testament, and experienced today in the lives of believers. The Messiah's redemptive power not only saves us from sin and death but also enables us to live under God's rule, experiencing His grace and bearing witness to His Kingdom.

10.2 Christ's Resurrection: The Ultimate Demonstration of God's Power

The resurrection of Jesus Christ is the central event in Christianity, embodying the ultimate display of God's power. As the crowning truth of the Gospel, it underscores the validity of Jesus' claim to divinity, the efficacy of His atoning sacrifice, and the assurance of our own resurrection and eternal life.

The Historical Reality of Christ's Resurrection

The New Testament presents the resurrection of Jesus Christ as a historical event, witnessed by numerous individuals. Paul, writing in the mid-first century C.E., provides the earliest written account of the resurrection, asserting that Christ "was raised on the third day in accordance with the Scriptures" and "appeared to Cephas, then to the twelve. Then he appeared to more than five hundred brothers at one time...Then he appeared to James, then to all the apostles. Last of all, as to one untimely born, he appeared also to me" (1 Corinthians 15:4-8, ESV).

The four Gospels offer detailed narratives of the resurrection, each providing unique yet complementary accounts of the event. These accounts include specific details such as the empty tomb (Matthew 28:6, ESV), the angelic announcement of Jesus' resurrection (Luke 24:5-6, ESV), and Jesus' post-resurrection appearances to His disciples (John 20:19-20, ESV).

These accounts establish the resurrection of Christ as a historical fact, not a mythical or symbolic narrative. This underscores the centrality of the resurrection to the Christian faith; as Paul declares, "if Christ has not been raised, your faith is futile and you are still in your sins" (1 Corinthians 15:17, ESV).

Christ's Resurrection as a Demonstration of God's Power

Christ's resurrection serves as a powerful demonstration of God's power, surpassing all human understanding and capabilities. It's noteworthy that in the New Testament, the power that raised Christ from the dead is often equated with the power of God at work in believers.

Paul, for instance, prays that the Ephesian believers may know "what is the immeasurable greatness of his power toward us who believe, according to the working of his great might that he worked in Christ when he raised him from the dead" (Ephesians 1:19-20, ESV).

In his letter to the Romans, Paul describes the believer's spiritual resurrection in baptism as being united with Christ in his death and resurrection, thereby highlighting the transformative power of God that brings about new life (Romans 6:3-5, ESV).

Christ's Resurrection as a Guarantee of our Resurrection and Eternal Life

Christ's resurrection is not an isolated event; it is a precursor and guarantee of our own resurrection and eternal life. As Paul declares, "But in fact Christ has been raised from the dead, the firstfruits of those who have fallen asleep. For as by a man came death, by a man has come also the resurrection of the dead. For as in Adam all die, so also in Christ shall all be made alive" (1 Corinthians 15:20-22, ESV).

Christ's resurrection is our assurance that death does not have the final word. Because He lives, we too will live. This hope of resurrection and eternal life is the believer's anchor, providing comfort in the face of death and motivation for godly living.

In conclusion, the resurrection of Jesus Christ is the ultimate demonstration of God's power, a pivotal event in human history that validates Christ's identity, confirms His redemptive work, and guarantees our future resurrection and eternal life. It epitomizes the Gospel message, encapsulating the hope, joy, and transforming power that define the Christian experience.

10.3 The Gift of Grace: God's Power to Save

The Bible presents the concept of grace as one of its central themes. Grace, in the biblical context, denotes God's unmerited favor and love towards humanity. It is His gift, given not because of anything we have done to earn it, but because of His abundant love and mercy. Grace is the means through which God exercises His power to save.

The Nature of God's Grace

God's grace is His unmerited favor, demonstrated supremely in the salvation provided through Jesus Christ. "For by grace you have been saved through faith. And this is not your own doing; it is the gift of God, not a result of works, so that no one may boast" (Ephesians 2:8-9, ESV). This passage emphasizes two crucial aspects of grace. First, grace is a gift from God, not something we earn. Second, grace is the means by which we are saved, through faith in Christ.

While humans are prone to think in terms of transactions and deserving, grace operates outside this paradigm. It is freely given, irrespective of merit, and it is expansive, covering all aspects of our relationship with God. It not only encompasses forgiveness and reconciliation but also sanctification, empowering us to live righteously (Titus 2:11-12, ESV).

Grace and the Old Testament

While the term "grace" appears more frequently in the New Testament, the concept permeates the Old Testament as well. It is woven into the fabric of God's interactions with His people, underscoring His forbearance, mercy, and steadfast love.

God's grace was evident in His covenant with Abraham, in which He promised to bless all nations through Abraham's offspring, despite Abraham's lack of merit (Genesis 12:1-3, ASV). Similarly, the Mosaic covenant, while conditioned on Israel's obedience, was initiated and maintained by God's grace. Israel's repeated failures underscored their inability to earn God's favor, yet He remained faithful, forgiving their sins and renewing His covenant with them (Exodus 34:6-7, ASV).

Grace and the New Covenant in Christ

With the advent of Christ, God's grace was revealed in its fullest extent. John 1:17 (ESV) states, "For the law was given through Moses; grace and truth came through Jesus Christ." Here, the contrast between the Mosaic Law and the grace offered through Christ is highlighted. While the law prescribed righteous living, it did not empower obedience. Conversely, grace not only provides the grounds for our justification but also empowers sanctified living.

Christ's life, death, and resurrection encapsulate God's grace. His sacrificial death, an unmerited act of love, provided the means for our salvation. His resurrection assures us of victory over sin and death, and His ascension and continual intercession provide us with an advocate before God (Romans 8:34, ESV).

The Implications of Grace

God's grace has profound implications for our lives. It liberates us from the burden of trying to earn God's favor and instills us with hope and confidence in our relationship with Him. Because of grace, our standing before God rests not on our performance but on Christ's finished work on the cross.

Moreover, grace empowers transformation. As Paul declares, "For the grace of God has appeared, bringing salvation for all people, training us to renounce ungodliness and worldly passions, and to live self-controlled, upright, and godly lives in the present age" (Titus 2:11-12, ESV). This sanctifying aspect of grace is God's power at work in us, enabling us to grow in godliness.

God's grace also necessitates a response from us. Since grace is received through faith, we must trust and rest in Christ's finished work for our salvation. Furthermore, having received such lavish grace, we are called to extend grace to others (Ephesians 4:32, ESV). As recipients of grace, we become conduits of God's grace in a broken world.

In conclusion, the gift of grace is central to God's power in salvation. It epitomizes His unmerited favor and love towards us and serves as the means by which we are saved and transformed. Through grace, God's power to save is marvelously displayed, assuring us of His unwavering commitment to our redemption. This divine commitment, enacted in grace, promises a sure and certain hope for all who trust in Christ, irrespective of their past. It offers a transformative power that leads us away from sin and towards righteousness, not through our strength, but through God's. The wonder of grace lies in its divine origin, its life-altering impact, and its availability to all who, in faith, turn towards Christ.

10.4 The Mind of Christ: God's Power in Our Lives

Having the mind of Christ refers to viewing life and its challenges from the same perspective as Jesus Christ. It means adopting His attitudes, thoughts, feelings, and actions. It includes understanding God's truths and applying them to daily life. This principle is crucial in understanding God's power in salvation and its practical implications in our lives.

Concept of the Mind of Christ in Scripture

The Apostle Paul introduces the concept of having the mind of Christ in his first letter to the Corinthians, stating, "For who has understood the mind of the Lord so as to instruct him? But we have the mind of Christ" (1 Corinthians 2:16, ESV). This verse comes after a lengthy discussion on wisdom and understanding, suggesting that having the mind of Christ is associated with wisdom and spiritual understanding.

Paul's mention of the mind of Christ implies an intimacy with God that goes beyond human understanding. This is not about achieving a state of divine knowledge or awareness, but rather a humble acceptance of God's wisdom and a willingness to obey His word.

Acquiring the Mind of Christ

The process of acquiring the mind of Christ is a lifelong journey of discipleship and transformation. It begins with a humble acknowledgment of our need for God and our inability to achieve righteousness on our own.

The primary means through which we acquire the mind of Christ is by immersing ourselves in Scripture, the inspired, inerrant Word of God. Paul exhorts, "Do not be conformed to this world, but be transformed by the renewal of your mind, that by testing you may discern what is the will of God, what is good and acceptable and perfect" (Romans 12:2, ESV). This verse suggests that the transformation of our mind—aligning it with the mind of Christ—occurs as we engage with and apply Scripture in our lives.

Implications of Having the Mind of Christ

Having the mind of Christ profoundly affects our lives. It transforms our perceptions, our values, and our behavior. It shapes our responses to life's trials, challenges, and blessings.

Adopting the mind of Christ leads to a life marked by humility, love, and obedience. In Philippians 2:5-8 (ESV), Paul outlines the self-sacrificial mindset that characterized Christ, "Have this mind among yourselves, which is yours in Christ Jesus, who... humbled himself by becoming obedient to the point of death, even death on a cross." Thus, the mind of Christ is marked by humility, love, and obedience to God's will.

The Mind of Christ in Practice

Practically, having the mind of Christ influences how we view and interact with others. It compels us to love our neighbors as ourselves, to forgive those who wrong us, and to seek justice for the oppressed. It prompts us to consider others more significant than ourselves, mirroring the humility of Christ.

Having the mind of Christ also changes how we approach suffering and trials. It enables us to see beyond our immediate circumstances, trusting in God's sovereignty and love. Just as Christ trusted the Father in His suffering, so we, too, learn to trust in our trials.

Furthermore, the mind of Christ directs us in decision-making. Rather than being swayed by worldly wisdom, we seek wisdom from above, discerning and adhering to God's will as revealed in His Word.

10.5 The Second Coming: God's Promised Future

The doctrine of the second coming of Christ is central to the Christian faith and is woven into the fabric of Scripture. Its study is crucial in understanding God's future promises and their implications for our lives.

Promise of the Second Coming

The New Testament is rich with verses speaking of Christ's return. In one of the most explicit instances, Jesus Himself promises, "And if

I go and prepare a place for you, I will come again and will take you to myself, that where I am you may be also" (John 14:3, ESV). Here, Jesus affirms His return, signaling it as an act of fulfilling His eternal promise of salvation. This promise is not only a cornerstone of Christian eschatology, but it also provides comfort and hope to believers.

Characteristics of the Second Coming

The second coming of Christ is described in a way that starkly contrasts with His first coming. While Jesus came in humility and obscurity the first time, His second coming will be grand and universally visible. "Behold, he is coming with the clouds, and every eye will see him, even those who pierced him, and all tribes of the earth will wail on account of him" (Revelation 1:7, ESV). The magnitude of this event underscores the fact that God's promises are not minor or ordinary; they are grand, monumental, and decisive.

The Second Coming and Judgment

The second coming of Christ is also closely associated with judgment. In Matthew 25:31-32 (ESV), Jesus describes His return in glory, saying, "When the Son of Man comes in his glory, and all the angels with him, then he will sit on his glorious throne. Before him will be gathered all the nations, and he will separate people one from another as a shepherd separates the sheep from the goats." Here, Jesus elucidates the sifting that will occur at His return, reinforcing the reality of divine justice and the importance of faithfulness.

Implications for Believers

The expectation of the second coming has profound implications for believers. It provides hope and encouragement, motivates godly living, and underscores the urgency of the Gospel mission.

The promise of Christ's return offers comfort and consolation to those suffering or experiencing hardship. It reassures believers of their future glory and the culmination of their salvation. The Apostle Paul, in 1 Thessalonians 4:18 (ESV), encourages believers with these words, "Therefore encourage one another with these words."

Moreover, the impending return of Christ motivates believers to live in righteousness and holiness. The Apostle John wrote, "And everyone who thus hopes in him purifies himself as he is pure" (1 John 3:3, ESV). The knowledge that Christ could return at any moment should inspire a life of faithfulness and dedication to God's commandments.

Furthermore, the imminent return of Christ underscores the urgency of spreading the Gospel. This sense of urgency can be found in Jesus' words: "We must work the works of him who sent me while it is day; night is coming, when no one can work" (John 9:4, ESV).

In conclusion, the promise of the second coming of Christ is a crucial aspect of God's future promises. It provides hope for believers, incites a life of holiness, and motivates evangelism. By studying this doctrine, we gain a deeper understanding of God's eternal plan and His power in salvation.

10.6 The New Jerusalem: God's Power in Our Eternal Hope

The New Jerusalem is a symbol of profound hope and the ultimate culmination of God's power in salvation. It is the biblical depiction of the final dwelling place of the redeemed, revealing God's glorious plan for those who remain faithful to the end.

The Promised New Jerusalem

The New Jerusalem is mentioned in the final chapters of the book of Revelation, where it is described as descending from God out of heaven. "And I saw the holy city, new Jerusalem, coming down out of heaven from God, prepared as a bride adorned for her husband" (Rev. 21:2, ESV). This depiction is symbolic of God's promise of a glorious eternal dwelling place for the redeemed, demonstrating His power in salvation and His covenant faithfulness.

The Characteristics of the New Jerusalem

The New Jerusalem is characterized by its immense beauty and grandeur, reflecting God's glory. John writes, "having the glory of God, its radiance like a most rare jewel, like a jasper, clear as crystal" (Rev. 21:11, ESV). The city is made of precious gems and pure gold, with gates of pearl, demonstrating the incomparable splendor of our eternal dwelling place.

The city's design also carries significance. Its square shape, equal in length, breadth, and height (Rev. 21:16, ESV), can be seen as symbolic of perfection and completion, resonating with the fullness of God's salvation plan.

God's Presence in the New Jerusalem

The most magnificent aspect of the New Jerusalem is the presence of God Himself. The city has no need for the sun or moon for the glory of God gives it light (Rev. 21:23, ESV). There is no temple, for God and the Lamb are its temple (Rev. 21:22, ESV). The direct and unhindered fellowship with God marks the ultimate fulfillment of our salvation. The promise of God's eternal presence offers Christians the hope of a time where they will see God face to face.

The New Jerusalem and the Nations

The New Jerusalem is also presented as a place of healing for the nations. "The leaves of the tree were for the healing of the nations" (Rev. 22:2, ESV). This demonstrates that God's eternal plan of salvation extends to all people and carries implications of peace, reconciliation, and harmony.

Implications for Believers

The New Jerusalem gives Christians a tangible vision of their eternal hope, motivating them to live righteously and passionately in this present life. It provides comfort to those suffering, knowing that their future residence is a place devoid of sorrow, pain, and death (Rev. 21:4, ESV).

Furthermore, the promise of the New Jerusalem inspires believers to share the Gospel message. With the knowledge of such a glorious eternal dwelling place, Christians are spurred to spread the good news of salvation to all, so others may also partake in this hope.

Finally, the promise of the New Jerusalem calls believers to a life of holiness. Revelation 21:27 (ESV) says, "But nothing unclean will ever enter it, nor anyone who does what is detestable or false, but only those who are written in the Lamb's book of life." This reinforces the Christian calling to live uprightly and walk in God's ways.

In summary, the New Jerusalem is the ultimate display of God's power in salvation and serves as our eternal hope. It provides comfort, inspires evangelism, and promotes holiness among believers. By focusing on the promise of the New Jerusalem, Christians can gain a deeper understanding of God's eternal plan and live in anticipation of its fulfillment.

BIBLIOGRAPHY

Andrews, Edward D. "*FAITHFUL MINDS: A Biblical and Cognitive Behavioral Therapy Approach to Mental Health and Wellness.*" Christian Publishing House, 2023.

Andrews, Edward D. "*MERE CHRISTIANITY REIMAGINED: Rediscovering the Faith for the 21st Century.*" Christian Publishing House, 2023.

Andrews, Edward D. "*UNSHAKABLE BELIEFS: Strategies for Strengthening and Defending Your Faith.*" Christian Publishing House, 2023.

Andrews, Edward D. "*YOU CAN MAKE A DIFFERENCE: Why and How Your Christian Life Makes a Difference.*" Christian Publishing House, 2017.

Andrews, Edward D. *"GOD WILL GET YOU THROUGH THIS: Hope and Help for Your Difficult Times.*" Christian Publishing House, 2017.

Andrews, Edward D. "*LET GOD USE YOU TO SOLVE YOUR PROBLEMS: GOD Will Instruct You and Teach You In the Way You Should Go.*" Christian Publishing House, 2018.

Piper, John. Desiring God, Revised Edition: Meditations of a Christian Hedonist. Multnomah, 2011.

Sproul, R.C. The Holiness of God. Tyndale Momentum, 2000.

Lewis, C.S. Mere Christianity. HarperOne, 2015.

Bridges, Jerry. The Pursuit of Holiness. NavPress, 2016.

Packer, J.I. Knowing God. InterVarsity Press, 2018.

Chan, Francis. Crazy Love: Overwhelmed by a Relentless God. David C. Cook, 2013.

Bonhoeffer, Dietrich. The Cost of Discipleship. Touchstone, 1995.

Keller, Timothy. The Reason for God: Belief in an Age of Skepticism. Penguin Books, 2009.

Lewis, C.S. The Problem of Pain. HarperOne, 2015.

Tozer, A.W. The Knowledge of the Holy: The Attributes of God: Their Meaning in the Christian Life. HarperOne, 2009.

Platt, David. Radical: Taking Back Your Faith from the American Dream. Multnomah, 2010.

Stott, John. The Cross of Christ. InterVarsity Press, 2006.

Keller, Timothy. Prayer: Experiencing Awe and Intimacy with God. Penguin Books, 2016.

Willard, Dallas. The Divine Conspiracy: Rediscovering Our Hidden Life In God. HarperOne, 1998.

MacArthur, John. The Gospel According to Jesus: What Is Authentic Faith? Zondervan, 2008.

Alcorn, Randy. Heaven. Tyndale Momentum, 2004.

Nouwen, Henri J.M. The Return of the Prodigal Son: A Story of Homecoming. Image, 1994.

Lucado, Max. Anxious for Nothing: Finding Calm in a Chaotic World. Thomas Nelson, 2017.

Eldredge, John. Wild at Heart: Discovering the Secret of a Man's Soul. Thomas Nelson, 2010.

Wiersbe, Warren. The Wiersbe Bible Commentary: The Complete Old Testament in One Volume. David C Cook, 2007.

www.ingramcontent.com/pod-product-compliance
Lightning Source LLC
Chambersburg PA
CBHW070448050426
42451CB00015B/3392